Village

An Affair with English Cricket

Tim Wade

TRAFFORD

Printed in Victoria, Canada

Note for Librarians: a cataloguing record for this book that includes Dewey Classification and US Library of Congress numbers is available from the National Library of Canada. The complete cataloguing record can be obtained from the National Library's online database at:
www.nlc-bnc.ca/amicus/index-e.html
ISBN 1-4120-2608-3

TRAFFORD

This book was published on-demand in cooperation with Trafford Publishing. On-demand publishing is a unique process and service of making a book available for retail sale to the public taking advantage of on-demand manufacturing and Internet marketing. On-demand publishing includes promotions, retail sales, manufacturing, order fulfilment,

accounting and collecting royalties on behalf of the author.

Suite 6E, 2333 Government St., Victoria, B.C. V8T 4P4, CANADA
Phone 250-383-6864   Toll-free 1-888-232-4444 (Canada & US)
Fax 250-383-6804   E-mail sales@trafford.com   Web site www.trafford.com
TRAFFORD PUBLISHING IS A DIVISION OF TRAFFORD HOLDINGS LTD.
Trafford Catalogue #04-0436   www.trafford.com/robots/04-0436.html

10   9   8   7   6   5   4   3   2   1

For Ruth
x

Contents

· 1 ·

How an Australian came to Turville Park Cricket Club, Henley-on-Thames, and what this means for the international cricket balance of power.

'The trouble with the rat race is, even if you win, you're still a rat.' **Lily Tomlin**

A few assorted terms which might be freely associated with cricket, in no particular order -

- ⊖ genial
- ⊖ traditional
- ⊖ venerable
- ⊖ scones
- ⊖ green
- ⊖ willow (the non-Buffy variety)
- ⊖ arcane
- ⊖ humility
- ⊖ touring
- ⊖ silly hats
- ⊖ silly-leg

These expressions probably go as close as anyone ever

will to capturing the essence of cricket - this strangest of pastimes.

So why not stop there? Why attempt to distill this essence ever more finely?

Because it's there (seems particularly relevant after celebrating the 50th anniversary year of the Everest conquest - by an antipodean, no less).

Because the game is beautiful, and inspires prose, both in the playing, and the telling (and re-telling).

Because my family still (bravely) struggles to understand why I practise these dark arts, week after week, year after year.

Because it's funny, in a sort of 'One Flew Over The Cuckoo's Nest' way.

But most importantly, because I can. After an interesting 20 year career in professional life (tax law) and business (banking and insurance) I elected to take a two year sabbatical, beginning in 2003, while based in London with my family. This included a Masters of Philosophy at Cambridge University, which inevitably spurred a bout of navel gazing.

Ruth, my wife, quietly worried that this was menopausal, and watched for the tell tale signs, like shopping for red sports cars. Silly of course. It was always going to be racing car green. My four children eventually got over the shock of having me around to help with their homework, and vet their boyfriends/girlfriends with 20 page questionnaires. But the real motivation for this time out was just that. Time out. To read. To worry about things other than Boards and Monthly Financial Reports. To spend more time with my family in this most remarkable

European capital. To play cricket (of course). And to write about it.

I love cricket, and have spent 33 years playing the game competitively. Cricket has produced, for me, some of life's richest experiences. Comic, romantic, tragic, noble, frustrating, uplifting. Sometimes all of them just in the space of time it takes at the start of a new season to try on last years cricket strides.

My three major 'home' clubs have been in Melbourne, Australia (St. Andrews Cricket Club), Singapore (Singapore Cricket Club), and now Henley, England (Turville Park Cricket Club). I have laboured with devotion and deep affection over wickets in Australia, New Zealand, Singapore, Malaysia, Thailand, Hong Kong, The Maldives, England and France. Until arriving in England in 2000, all of my cricket had been of the ultra-competitive, limited overs variety. As you might expect, my apprenticeship in Australia was very much of the 'fight to the death' variety. Village cricket is more of the 'death to the fight' strain.

Like Nick Hornby in the Introduction to his and Nick Coleman's compilation of 'Sports Writing', I essentially agree that sport 'does not exist to enlighten. It exists to be experienced.' Cricket is obviously not a metaphor for life. But it can nevertheless be a powerful exemplar and teacher. It has been an unambiguously positive influence on my life, and the source for many, many friends from around the world who are like-minded in their almost eccentric devotion to this game.

In this spirit of pseudo-philosophical inquiry, the following diary, or series of essays - of three years with my adopted English village team, Turville Park - attempts to answer some of the big questions which cricketers grapple with on a routine basis ('who forgot the bloody score-book?', 'who nicked the last sausage roll?' and 'was W.G Grace a better batsman than Sachin Tendulkar because he played before the invention of velcro?').

The insights revealed in this diary are in large part a reflection of my 33 years of accumulated cricketing delights and frustrations, set against the backdrop of a perfectly idyllic village cricket competition in and around Henley from 2001 to 2003. In many senses, Turville Park Cricket Club is the vehicle for these musings, and I want to thank my TPCC team mates for being such entertaining fellow travellers.

I first came to Turville through the good offices of Barnaby Bazell (Haileybury and Cambridge), a dear friend who I had first met when we played cricket together in Singapore for three years in the period 1988-1990. We enjoyed no little success representing the famed Singapore Cricket Club, where the curries, and the touring, were special features of cricket life in this post-colonial outpost. Cricket was one of the last vestiges of the Stamford Raffles generation which the Singaporeans had yet to get around to banning. This made cricket more resilient in Singapore than both chewing gum and free speech. It was so much richer for this. I was privileged to Captain the SCC in 1989 when we managed to win all three titles on offer. Barnaby was my wicket keeper and conscience, helping me to smooth out some of the rough Australian edges.

Barney is an archetypal eccentric, and so defies ready

categorisation or even description. Some flavour is probably important as he is a regular feature in these pages, so I hope the following random thoughts serve. He is now 50, but first looked it fifteen years ago, when I first met him. He is a keen sports lover - cricket, rugby union, golf and football in particular. He loves tramping about in the woods in his native Oxfordshire with his daughters, and collecting mushrooms.

He travels widely and regularly, and loves food. Any food. He wears sarongs around the house. This frightened my children. A lot. Finally, he won a Blue at Cambridge for boxing. Both Barnaby, and Felicity his wife, had become good friends in Singapore, and were especially generous to us when we decided to move to London in 2000 (helping with such things as schools, TV licences, Arsenal Membership packs with pre-completed application forms). When Barnaby invited me to join his local village team, I did not hesitate for a moment. If these chaps were able to put up with Barnaby's eccentricities, then they must love their cricket very much indeed.

While I was not a complete stranger to Turville Park Cricket Club, having guested for the team in 1998 on one of my frequent visits to London, there was certainly a probationary period for me as I began to get known around the Club. Turville is a Henley based team, and members coming from *London* are regarded as exotic. The prospect of a newcomer from 10,000 miles further south therefore took some getting used to. Moreover, here I was - an Australian - and a fully paid up, card carrying member of The Old Enemy. Australia had been England's nemesis in international cricket competition for almost 20 years now, and its fiercest rival for over 120 years. There has always been something special about the cricketing relationship between our two nations, usually illustrated by episodes like Bodyline. An even more telling reflection lies in the remarkable fact that Bradman, Barnes, Miller and Morris all enjoyed higher Test Match averages against England than in any other form of the game. More recently, Steve Waugh has managed an average just on 50 at Test level, but this is after accounting for a career average of nearly 60 against England.

In any event, I eventually managed to break down the traditional English reserve through a combination of suffering the local (warm) bitter - Brakspears; even-ing out my vowels; introducing my team mates to Ruth (always a sure fire way to charm new friends); and nodding approvingly when the discussion turned to England's last great cricket victory over Australia, at Headingley in 1981. This last occurred roughly every five minutes.

Perhaps even more importantly, I managed to register a couple of decent scores, and even exhibited a willingness to serve up some slow medium pace bowling. Oddly, I often seemed to find myself being called on for these duties straight after tea break, when most sensible English gentlemen were still digesting an extravagant number of scones.

Let me take a moment to describe the setting in which we were lucky enough to play. Our ground at Turville Heath is about six miles outside Henley-on-Thames on the Buckinghamshire/Oxfordshire border. My approach route was along a narrow single track lane, through the quiet hamlet of Northend, and past properties called 'Overdale', 'Pennlands' and 'Badgerbury' - names that would be impossibly twee if this wasn't genuine 'Wind In The Willows' country. The ground is set well back from the road behind some reasonably dense forest, on the estate of Lord Sainsbury of Turville, a serving Labor Minister, and eponymously famous for the supermarket chain. Lord Sainsbury inherited the Turville ground arrangements when he acquired the estate in 1996 and continues to support the Cricket Club in splendid style.

The setting is strictly speaking more rural than traditionally 'village'. The views are sweeping as we enjoy an elevated position in the Chilterns which Constable would have delighted in (assuming, of course, that he was prepared to bowl up the hill). The sky feels very, very 'big' here. The ground itself slopes gently away and down to the barley fields which ring more than one-half of the field. Summer time provides the wonderful sight of barley stalks ready for harvest growing up to seven feet tall. It also results in much cursing if the ball happens to travel outside the boundary and disappear amongst the undergrowth. (Local Knowledge Tip Number 1 : this is often a useful way to slow the progress of a dominant opposing batsman. After he has lobbed one into the foliage, sometimes up to six or seven Turville fielders join the 'search' as they do little more than mill about out of sight discussing the latest England Test Captain to resign in tears.)

The ground is circled by a sturdy metal fence, which lends a special but slightly strange air of cricketing authenticity and authority (as if to make it clear that the cows and

13

sheep have no playing rights whatsoever). On the top side, the field is flanked by a functional if unspectacular pavilion, with the mandatory flag pole. Further around the boundary is the massive sycamore tree which provides the Club with its emblem. The tree has stood magnificently in its position just inside the boundary line for upwards of 150 years. Even today, there is no certainty about the rules regarding balls which are struck into the tree. These things obviously take time.

The cricket wicket itself is gorgeous, and the envy of all our neighbours and other visitors. Flat, true, and with just enough grass, it is lovingly maintained by two passionate club members.

The overall aesthetic is complemented (naturally) by rolling fields, populated by unhurried livestock (mostly sheep, with their ever so gently mocking 'baa's'), the occasional farm or manor house peeping out from behind tree cover, and a nearby mature forest, housing amongst other things the local red kite community. The kite is a magnificent species of bird which uses its wingspan of up to five feet to glide effortlessly above our much more sedentary efforts on the cricket field. At the same time, planes which have left Heathrow, and reached their cruising altitude of 30,000 feet, are describing arcs with their vapour trails that can reach from one horizon to the other. It is not unusual to miss one or two balls in a match whilst admiring these spectacles. This rarely matters, unless you happen to be umpiring at the time.

The Annual Ground fee levied by Lord Sainsbury for this picture postcard version of cricket nirvana runs to the princely (lordly?) sum of one 'peppercorn'. The lease agreement does require Turville cricketers to stand back three times every year should Lord Sainsbury wish to land his helicopter on the ground. This seems the very least we can do. Please keep shopping at Sainsbury's. I assume that by now they must at least have a modest supply of peppercorns in stock.

The Club's fixture card was, well, a fixture, and typically saw Turville playing in 35 games in a season, against essentially same teams on the same dates. The second Chapter picks up with the final game of my first year at Turville in Season 2001 against West Wycombe, and the last Chapter finishes with the annual intra club game at Wormsley Estate, the ground of the late John Paul Getty II, at the end of season 2003.

At this point, a health warning. I must caution against any expectations of drama in the outcomes of our weekly struggles. No League Tables, no cumulative win/loss ratio analysis, and no desperate, last gasp battles to stave off relegation. This may be considered somewhat unAustralian, and I have wondered whether I must hand in my passport at the Australian High Commission, or submit to retraining in Earls Court, or even at the Australian Cricket Academy (do they run 'World Cricket Domination' as a core subject or an elective?). But no, this is Declaration Cricket. It is played at a gentle pace, usually on Sundays. We start at two, but the fixture card might just as well read '2.00 for 2.30'. There are very few aspirants for higher cricket duties at Turville - the England Cricket Team might be said to have its full quota of broken down hacks in any event.

Although described loosely as a Diary, there is also a distinct lack of chronological structure in the following notes. I use games from Seasons 2001-2003 in a random order to help illustrate the themes which I want to explore. In this way, I hope to provide some context for understanding just why cricket is so revered in such a remarkably diverse assortment of communities around the world. I do not set out to glorify a faux-naif 'dreaming spires' vision of village cricket; however, if it looks like that at times then it is essentially as I have found it. I'm more than happy to mock the game, its customs, and its practitioners, but the environment is very, very real. I also accept that there must be different strains of village cricket. For example, I simply haven't found Marcus Berkmann's village cricket setting (in his clever and quirky 'Rain Men') where 'every team is riven by internal disputes of every imaginable kind', and 'everyone goes to the considerable effort of cheating each other at every turn'. But I hope there is enough commonality in the following to resonate in pubs across different communities.

And so, on with the sabbatical, and these humble cricket thoughtpieces. Alert readers will already have guessed that the pretexts for this frolic which I have described above are all as skinny as they sound. This has everything to do with recapturing the glories of lost student days, and more particularly in my case, providing an excuse to wear a tweed coat, smoke a pipe, and play (as well as pontificate on) sport with a slightly more raffish crowd than I had been accustomed to in my formative cricketing years on the matting wicketed dustbowls of Melbourne.

·2·

Cricket ... Why, Exactly?

Turville Park Cricket Club v. West Wycombe,
Sunday, 23 September, 2001

'Cricket - a game which the English, not being
a spiritual people, have invented in order to give
themselves some conception of eternity.'
Lord Mancroft

September. Cold. The last match of the 2001 season. A good turnout, as we are all starting to worry about the looming winter break, and the impact this enforced hibernation will have on us as finely tuned athletes (Turville's average age for this game is unhealthily north of 40). What becomes of modest fitness levels? Do they become immodest? Brazen?

Our captain for the day is Barnaby, as our regular skipper, Paul Girdler, is having a week off. Paul is in love, which is delightful, but she is not a cricket fan. He is therefore going through that elaborate mating ritual of marking out the importance of cricket in his life, and his unstinting devotion to the cause of Turville Park Cricket Club. In other words, he has said nothing, and has completely abandoned us for sex. He'll come around.

Barnaby wins the toss and inserts the opposition on a

soggy wicket in a light drizzle (given it is our last game, we would probably have played in a monsoon). The decision to bat is largely a matter of self defence, as the wicket behaves alarmingly, and our rather pedestrian attack looks unfeasibly threatening.

One of the features of playing on turf wickets in England is of course their unpredictability. One of the features of bowling on these wickets is, as any part time bowler will tell you, to take full credit for this unpredictability. It is a noble art, depicting - largely through elaborate gestures and pained facial expressions - the enormous skill you have just employed in causing a ball to deviate off a ridge on the pitch which the part-time groundsman has simply failed to roll out. In truth, you know you should be grateful simply to have pitched the ball somewhere in the batsman's vicinity.

After a few desultory overs of bowling on my part, during which time my theatrics fail to dislodge (much less entertain) any opposing batsmen, I am relieved of duty and find myself once again gazing at England. The setting is a snug field in the hollow of a gently sloping valley in the high achieving County of Buckinghamshire. The ground is incongruously positioned nearby to the 'Hellfire Caves', a local tourist attraction of deep underground passages created by the founder of the notorious Hellfire Club. A sign on the approach to the ground heightens the incongruity to almost surreal levels, as it advertises the 'Hellfire Caves and Tea Rooms'. I'm not making this up. ('Another scone, Prince of Darkness?')

On this afternoon, the light rain enhances the green-ness

of the vista at the West Wycombe ground, and there are the statutory sheep grazing contentedly on the hillside. The nearby estate manor is large, but slightly austere, with what look like battlements. With the Romans safely accounted for, I imagine that perhaps these defences are designed to ward off the ever encroaching British motorways. I could be wrong.

It is at this point that I am observing the time honoured practice of wondering 'what on earth am I doing here?' It's cold. The cricket is unremarkable. My family is happy and warm at home. I have a million things to agonise over ahead of a busy week at work (I am still a stressed out *salaryman* at this stage). Then, in the middle of an English field, after more than 30 years of unquestioning devotion to this whimsical game, the answer presents itself. While I'm confident that many before me have uncovered this simplest of truths, most likely more rapidly than me, it is quite a Damascene moment. Not altogether religious perhaps, but can it be a co-incidence that - at the same time - the rain lifted, a distinct glow suffused the valley, and a West Wycombe batsman stepped on his own wicket to give us the breakthrough we were looking for? The surprising thing is that my discovery didn't mature over time. It just arrived. I almost expected the animated God from Monty Python's 'Holy Grail' to appear in the sky and say brusquely 'Of course it's a good game!'

I enjoy cricket because it is unhurried, gentle (in the sense that that word informs the term 'gentleman'), gracious, and slightly quirky. In the main, these are not features of an otherwise stressful modern existence.

19

Perhaps most importantly, a game of cricket *forces* you to relax. You are a captive, not *audience* (anyone can watch sport), but *participant* in this activity. I can't make a mobile phone call, or check my emails, or read a newspaper, or agitate over the next exciting new instalment of 'teenage rearing'. I am a happy and willing part of an activity that is in turn part game, part leisure activity, part art, part contest, part psychotherapy, part theatre and part cultural experience. The game requires just enough concentration to keep out unwelcome workaday contemplations, but not so much that you could possibly overlook the charm of your surroundings. I suspect that there is also something just a little liberating about pursuing an activity which is so obviously 'cult-ish' in public, and in broad daylight.

Although overwhelmingly languid, there can still be moments in cricket when tensions rise and the adrenalin courses through the veins ('can I balance a sandwich while holding both a scone and a cup of tea at the same time?'). But much of the charm of cricket lies in the reversion to long periods of enforced solitude, with the opportunity to reflect on how to turn your epiphany into a money making book writing exercise.

While not critical to the enjoyment of cricket, during quieter moments like this I often find myself pondering exactly what 'it' is. Terms like 'sport' and 'game' are functional, but seem inadequate in properly describing cricket. 'Contest' is better because it captures wider notions - not only the physical exertions, but also the battle of wills, and the struggle with oneself. But in the end, this phrase is a little too gladiatorial. 'Pursuit' is too bland, 'Undertaking' too grim, 'Endeavour' a bit too workmanlike. On balance, I decide to settle on 'Affair'. While it contains a number of different connotations, for me there is enough of a hint of romance, elegance, action and business to portray the richness of cricket. So, every week I cheerfully explain to Ruth that I am off to pursue my affair with cricket. Every so often I'm sure she wonders if this is code for something silly. She's right of course, but it's no code.

Compare cricket with almost any other team sport, and its uniqueness becomes even clearer. It is possible to spend six hours engaged in a cricket game, sometimes with as little as just a few minutes of truly active physical involvement. That cricketers put up with such a low 'reward' for effort ratio means there must almost by definition be a wider appeal in taking part in the game. While this is not a justification in itself, it is nevertheless a remarkable detail, especially when the game's extended playing time makes it so unfriendly to partners and families.

Other sports, like football, tennis, squash, bowls, basketball, baseball (for example) all require close attention from each member of the team, over a much more concentrated period of time. This is fine, but robs these sports of any real mental therapeutic value. Even golf demands consistent and constant physical activity (usually of a particularly unrelaxing kind). Other pursuits - say fishing - may compare in terms of their 'sedentar-iness' but typically fail to capture either the team oriented spirit of cricket, or what might be described as its 'noble lassitude' (you understand I am now fully immersed in my 'romantic' phase. That's as Neville Cardus as it gets for now).

Many view the sheer lack of productivity and obvious 'reward' from cricket as daft (see above, the 'what on earth am I doing here' camp). But it's actually part of the point. Even if I'm wrong, the next nearest form of 'activity' that I can think of would involve lying in a hammock for six hours, and then going to the pub for a few beers with some mates.

There's no way Ruth is going to let me get away with that ...

●

West Wycombe managed to compile just 120 runs in very difficult conditions. Turville was happily able to overtake this total before the darkness descended, both over the ground, and over Season 2001.

At the end of my first year in England, I had found a new home, and made some new friends. But I had only just begun the task of unravelling the mystery of village cricket. Who knows, perhaps there was a sinister side simmering unseen below the surface? (you know the sort of thing - fake cream on the scones?, beer watered down at the pub?, barley fields hiding a massive marijuana crop?). I somehow doubted it, but was determined to find the truth.

·3·

The Language of Cricket

Turville v. Stonor, Sunday 18 August, 2002

'I don't like to think of it as sledging.
I prefer the phrase "mental disintegration".'
Steve Waugh

I love that Australia's Test Cricket Captain regards the phrase 'mental disintegration' as a kinder, gentler description of the Australian team's efforts at on-field discourse. You would have liked him to have fronted the Bush Administration's PR in Iraq ('Oh sure we had overwhelming superiority, but we needed to crush the opposition in order to maintain our record breaking winning streak. Oh, and lay off Warnie will you guys - nothing's been proved yet').

The rules in village cricket are of course a little different. Turville's local derby against neighbouring Stonor provides a perfect backdrop to explore some of the peculiar vernacular, euphemism and nomenclature which attends the sport. It also shows how an unsuspecting traveller needs to take special care with the use of the language in a foreign country. The cricket priesthood has subtle but significant variations in tongues around the world.

While not quite Pakistan v. India, Yorkshire v. Lancashire, or Victoria v. New South Wales, the Turville v. Stonor fixture has a larger than usual amount of 'ginger' for this otherwise sleepy village competition. The genesis of this competitiveness is not entirely clear, but some of the prevailing spice is provided, in theory at least, by the Hunts, *pere et fils*. This local farming family has produced in father Richard, a gracious and determined stalwart of the Stonor Cricket Club, and in son James, Turville's tearaway opening bowler, powerful middle order bat and Vice-Captain. This is no Corleone clan, riven with violent internal ructions however. A nicer family you simply couldn't wish to meet. Jamie is in fact Turville's answer to Doris Day. Impossibly nice, enormously, casually talented and unconscionably modest. James is also the last of four children, and the only boy. He is the original prodigal son. Richard in turn is a gentleman farmer and cricketer. If these guys were to have anything to do with it, the scene was obviously set for a major outbreak of 'Oh, well played's'.

As you might imagine, Stonor worthies make regular overtures to James to return to the bosom of his familial Club. But Jamie is having none of it. The decision he made to come to Turville was deliberate, considered and mature. He was all of 11 at the time. Turville was prepared to offer young James a regular game, while Stonor was not. This is as close as Turville has ever come to a pro-active 'youth policy'. The next step in the Club's detailed development plan sees it anxiously awaiting the progeny of James' recent betrothal to his wife Felicity.

Before turning to the Stonor match, it might be helpful

24

to offer some thoughts on sledging. At the outset, as an Australian, I was expected by my Turville team mates to be loud and offensive (a sort of Ian Chappell meets Les Patterson stereotype). They were relieved (I think) to discover that I was nothing of the kind, although they did continue to instinctively look to me first if there were any prats on the opposing team who needed 'verballing'. I never quite figured out how to react to this, so my response was typically a confused, muffled, embarrassed noise which I suspect sounded a little like a belligerent budgie. My reticence to sledge was so surprising to some, that a routine business trip which I made back to Australia during the year was assumed to be for re-programming ('Sledging For The Mature Aged Cricketer'?).

Sledging is unacceptable. There can be no justification for personal insults on the field, at least in this form of the game. It is the complete antithesis to the charm and grace that so distinguishes cricket. Like many Australians, I am simultaneously awed by the dominant contemporary Australian Test Teams, whilst being embarrassed by their boorishness, most particularly in dead rubber games. For plain silliness, it is hard to go past the thinking that says abuse 'stays on the field' and everyone can be friends again off the field. The very last person I want to share a beer with is someone who has just been deliberately rude to me and/or my forbears. In what other pursuit or walk of life is this tolerable? (Naturally, I exclude football referees from this analysis on the basis that they are congenitally and universally inept, and deserve everything they get.) In his revealing study of the English County Cricket treadmill

('A Lot of Hard Yakka'), Simon Hughes talks about the oddness of Ian Botham and Dean Jones shifting from 'mortal combat' (in the World Cup) to 'bosom pals' (at Durham) within the space of a month. Hughes concludes simply that 'most exhibitionists practise this kind of duplicity'. Well maybe, but in the amateur form of the game, it is simply naff.

So, for those of you who are unsure, here is a semi-comprehensive list of what you can and cannot say in the heat of battle -

Sledging

⊖ 'F--- off, you plonker'

⊖ 'Is it conceivable that you might essay a cricket shot any time soon?' (the English equivalent of the all-purpose Australian sledge 'Jeez you're crap')

⊖ 'What does your husband say about you borrowing his trousers today?'

⊖ 'We're down to the tail now lads' (this to the opposing number 3 batsman who has just arrived at the wicket). Not really a sledge, but so unimaginative as to warrant contempt.

⊖ 'So I see the $A is now down to only 34 pence' (this is an intelligent, but unnecessarily cruel sledge, which I have no intention of forgiving)

Sportsmanship

⊖ 'Come on lads, we're due a wicket' (even when uttered directly at the batsman from two feet away, using the third person plural always has a distinctly ameliorating affect)

⊖ 'Come on [insert team name here]' (not strictly sledging, more to remind the captain that you are awake)

⊖ 'Come on [insert bowler's name here]' (this is actually often a sledge at said bowler, and also useful for encouraging the captain to give you a bowl, instead of persevering with the tripe currently being served up)

⊖ 'Straight out to cow corner, please John' (this within earshot of the incoming 'slogger'). Can also be used as a sledge when directed at an incoming 'plodder'.

For my part, there is an over-riding guiding principle. It's important to be funny. This is a game which, because of its rituals and formalities, requires regular piss taking, so we are reminded not to take ourselves too seriously.

The language of cricket fascinates in many other ways. The following themes are just some of those which have tickled my fancy in England.

Mid-pitch conversations

When two batsmen meet mid-pitch between overs, I am always intrigued by what they say. There is often an irresistible urge to share inanities. Englishmen who normally trade in monosyllables are suddenly bursting with animated prose. Generally, the conversation will go one of two ways - 'This guy is drifting away and seaming in, so be careful not to play inside, and watch the man at extra, he's deep, so we might steal one'. Not only is this completely unintelligible to the lay population, but it is almost always diabolically unhelpful advice. Alternatively, there is the 'So is it the Fox and Hounds or The Crown tonight?' form of discourse. This is at least interesting and relevant, but not as you are straining every nerve end not to get out on a pitch which doesn't seem to have had any acquaintance with a roller for over a month. I confess I disdain the practice of building social occasions on the wicket during an innings, so I deliberately avoid them by performing elaborate and entirely unnecessary gardening exercises on the pitch, so as not to catch my partner's eye. 'Rude Australian' I'm sure they're thinking. 'Schizophrenic Englishman' I think in reply.

Modesty

I like that this game inspires modesty in most players. In England, it is almost absurdly exaggerated (to paraphrase Churchill on Clement Attlee, English cricketers might be said to have an awful lot to be modest about). Just one example - this, to Colin Simon, Turville's Treasurer and opening batsman, who scored 100 in his last innings - 'So, how did you do last week, Colin?' Modest Colin - 'Not so bad, I managed to take some of the shine off the ball'. There is little testosterone, less boasting, and much gracious self effacement. I accept that this is not a rule of universal application (see St Johns East Malvern First XI, 1990-1994, Melbourne South Suburban League. Tossers.)

Taboo Words

According to the 2003 edition of the 'Collins English Dictionary', only sixteen words remain 'taboo' in the English language. Since the 2000 Edition, the editors have downgraded as many as seventy words (for example, 'bollocks') from taboo to 'slang'. I would suggest that there nevertheless remain a number of additional terms or phrases which are not suitable for sensitive English ears in village cricket circles. These include 'Warne' (and never run this together with 'Gatting' in the same sentence) and 'the tea (or the beer) is cold'.

Equally, there are taboos in Australia and Singapore which cricket lovers in those countries should be alert for. In Australia, 'bollocks' is of course a term of endearment, so there are not many rules to keep in mind. Nevertheless, you should never utter the words 'I declare', or 'sorry' (remember, Australians are a race who, it was once observed, only ever 'walk' if the elevator has broken down). For Singapore, the rules are less cricket specific. It is forbidden to say out loud, 'recession' (this is a go-getting island economy after all) and 'universal suffrage' (not critical for the economic miracle it would seem).

•

The match against Stonor sadly turned into a one-sided affair, with our arch rivals maintaining their recent record of superior performances. Turville struggled to 141, and Stonor comfortably overhauled this total for the loss of only four wickets. Perhaps the 'high' point for me came when I uttered a genuine cry of pleasure at the dismissal of a key Stonor batsman. I rendered this exclamation in the common Australian argot as 'You Pisser!' You must understand that this dismissal gave us the barest whiff of a chance of victory. When combined with my genetic dislike of losing,

I was perhaps guilty of celebrating a little too exuberantly. The departing batsman took all this in and, regrettably, heard my exclamation as 'Piss Off'. Not surprisingly, he took umbrage. Through the services of an interpreter, the misunderstanding was cleared up, and happily the offended batsman did in fact piss off.

The 'Henley Standard' match report was unusually scathing about the need for Turville to lift its standards in order to restore the lustre to this ancient contest. But in a sign that the chronicler was perhaps not entirely on top of his journalistic game, I was described as the 'improving Tim Wade' (for my 44).

It's nice to be improving at age 43. I'm expecting a Test team call-up by the time I reach 52 on this measure, if I can just improve on my 'F....ing' and 'Blinding' ...

·4·

'It's Character Building'
Turville v. Hambleden, Sunday, 24 May, 2003 ·

'Cricket's a symbol of life, and the world's woe in little
... with what I most enjoy, contented least.'
**Hugh de Selincourt's fictional Cricket Captain, Paul
Gauvinier, in "The Cricket Match"**

Cricket is a pastime that sorely tests one's resolve to maintain equability, in the face of circumstances which can be overwhelmingly trying. The beauty of cricket is that you are able to almost instantly forgive it, and turn up the next week for further renovation work on your obviously still deficient character.

Against Hambleden, I was faced with a quite typical example of how time, misfortune and cricket's unyielding rules can conspire to produce a humility bolstering after-noon.

For this encounter, we were only able to marshal 10 of the required 11 players. One of London's seemingly endless Bank Holiday weekends (English public's motto: 'Hate the Banks, Love the Holidays') meant that our talent pool had been seriously depleted. No doubt all those missing players with their fancy excuses (Paris, Prague, Palermo etc.) would return after their weekends away, tortured by their freshly depleted moral fibre (and hopefully a good dose of sunburn).

The skipper, Paul Girdler, lost the toss, and we found ourselves in the field on an unseasonably muggy May day. It was the stillness on this afternoon which inspired a special serenity, prompting a good deal of wistful gazing into the middle distance at the early signs of spring growth in the nearby barley fields, red kites soaring majestically overhead, and Barnaby's typically improbable garb of cream jumper with pink piping, orange wicket keepers gloves, black cap (Singapore Cricket Club) and dusty boots dating from some time around the Boer War.

Our collective reverential introspection lasted about five or six minutes, at which point the Hambleden bats began a most uncivil onslaught. The ball was dispatched to all parts of the field - bigger by one-eleventh given our missing team mate, but feeling like one-half larger in view of our under-manned and overwhelmed bowling attack. Mercifully, afternoon tea arrived, and our opponents did the decent thing by declaring their innings closed having run up 225 runs in only 41 overs.

No matter. We had a good batting side, and the skipper was confident of overtaking the Hambleden total. We never got close. After struggling to 142 runs, the game petered out into a tame draw, as Hambleden had only dismissed six of our ten batsmen. Unusually, and unfortunately, Hambleden declined to open up the game with some slower bowling in order to achieve a result. This was of course in direct contravention of the Geneva Convention, and Cherie Blair was subsequently engaged to make our Human Rights case.

The fact that 126 man hours, or more than three working weeks, had been expended on this match *without* producing a result might be considered frustrating enough (for more on this, see Chapter 5 'Declaration Cricket - Noble Art or Magnificent Con?'). But the real morale sapping and character building for me was defined by my paltry contribution - a mere five minutes of batting over the course of a long, hot afternoon. As near to a 'fresh air' game as one can get. While I have elsewhere lauded the merits of solitude, there is of course a limit. Against Hambleden, I just needed a long beard and vestments to be transformed into a Trappist Monk. I wondered if I should re-introduce myself to my team mates at the end of proceedings.

Batting at number three, and in good touch after a solid pre-season training program (no, really), I smashed a six with my first scoring shot, courtesy of a long hop bearing a gilt edged invitation. Following this with two quick 4's, I made the usual mistake of thinking, just for the merest fraction of a second, that all my accumulated career heartbreaks would be washed away with a match winning century in record time. I hate how the game does this. Sure enough, I drilled the next ball down the throat of the fieldsman at point.

If the fieldsman had had any sense, he would have executed the typical Sunday afternoon manoeuvre of so contorting one's body as to appear to be interested in taking the catch, while cleverly crashing to the ground the instant after the ball has disappeared off in the direction of the boundary. At this point, one's team mates are then obliged to utter one of two things - 'Good effort, John' (if your gymnastics have been even barely plausible), or 'Come on lads, let's pick up our fielding' (if the ball has still managed to hit you on the boot, even as you pirouetted for safety). My chap did none of this, but stood stock still as I delivered the ball fiercely, but neatly, into his cupped hands. Out. You fool. The pitch was perfect. The bowling unprepossessing. You've let the captain down, the team down, not to mention the massive blow to your own ego and self worth.

Immediately, the mental tools are unholstered, and the necessary reconstruction work begins on your battered pride. It took me probably 20 years before I stopped hurling things (bats, gloves, expletives) once I had returned to the change rooms in these circumstances. While this might seem like (belated) maturity, I like to think that it has more to do with enriching the frustration, and the value of the ensuing character building experience. The only other experience which has since provoked a similar feeling of wanting to do spontaneous physical harm to something is of course British Rail 'service'.

After quickly achieving the sanctuary of the pavilion *without* anyone saying 'You plonker' (this has of course never happened in my career, but weirdly it seems always something to be feared), I prefer solitude. Largely because I am embarrassed by my efforts, but also because this is inevitably a private affair. Cricket is of course one of the most unforgiving of mistresses. The fact that I have no further opportunities to redeem myself for the rest of the afternoon adds a dimension to my suffering which is 'cruel and unusual' on almost any measure. There are many, many ways in which cricket can bring you low: dropping the opposition batsman - who goes on to make a match winning 100 - when he was on 0; bowling the last over of a game and conceding 12 runs, when the opposition only needed 10 runs to win; turning up late to an important match, at the wrong ground, without having packed your boots. It is the suddenness and finality which are so crucial to the humbling experience.

One of my favourite Turville stories (definition: concerns someone other than me) of humility through hardship involves none other than Barnaby. In one of our Derby games against Stonor, Barnaby was efficiently attending to his wicket keeping duties, when he was called upon to chase down a skied catch which had been launched by an opposition batsman high in the air, and 20 yards away to his left. The bowler, Paul Girdler, looked anxiously, but confidently, in Barnaby's direction, as our hero began to prepare himself for the task of completing this crucial dismissal. As part of these preliminaries, Barnaby took the traditional precaution of knocking his floppy cap from his head - the better to concentrate on the approaching missile with an unobstructed field of vision. This proved to be Barnaby's undoing, as he simultaneously emancipated his glasses from their previously secure resting place on his nose. At once, Barnaby was rendered essentially impotent. Not only was he unable to track the remaining trajectory of the now rapidly descending ball, but he was afraid to move one way or the other, for fear of treading on his expensive prescription glasses. From a distance, it appeared as if he had suddenly been struck dumb with fear, and decided not to attempt an interception of the projectile, which - it must be said - had reached such a height that at least three other fielders could have made the catch, none of whom had made the slightest movement in Barnaby's direction. The ball duly landed safely, just three feet further to Barnaby's left. As one, the rest of us thanked our lucky stars that we had been allowed to witness this elaborately, exquisitely, embarrassing moment for a man who now straps his glasses firmly to his head. No Stonor wicket could ever have been as valuable as this experience.

After about 10-15 minutes of ritualistic hand wringing and teeth gnashing after getting out against Hambleden (of the 'Why do I BOTHER with this?' variety) a sense of calm descends. The cricket gods obviously spend a good deal of time ministering to wounded souls, and it works a treat (well they do owe me big time after that catch). This is as close to a spiritual experience as I can think of. Despite being a rather indifferent agnostic, on some occasions I am almost convinced that there is a greater being meting out cricket success and failure based upon good deeds and Christian thoughts. This is more a matter of superstition than anything else. Indeed, the experience is probably most akin to the ancient Greco-Roman philosophy of Stoicism - virtuous individuals (that's me, quietly contemplating my sorry efforts), civic duty (well, I do manage to restrain myself from trashing the streets of Henley-on-Thames), and faith in a universal reason (there's no other way to explain why I endure this peculiar brand of torment). It is still no doubt presumptuous of me to pretend to appreciate stoicism without having supported England at football or cricket.

Back on the terrestrial plane, it is time for me to

move into the next phase - penance. You know the type, 'please skipper, can I umpire for 20 overs? score? come round to your place tomorrow and mow your lawns?' These reparations are inevitably never quite enough, and the sacrifice of a small furry specimen of local livestock would be the next logical step, if only we didn't have their proprietors so near to hand.

Sadly, this process has been all too frequent for me, which of course means that my character should now be of almost Mandela-esque proportions. But I'm sure my experience is just the merest echo of similar episodes occurring up and down the country each weekend. And of course I am not suggesting that this is in the same category as Hillary (Edmund, or Clinton) for the sheer testing of wills. Several days later, I find I am still ruing my efforts against Hambleden. Despite this, I am strangely, perversely, feeling good about the game of cricket. The laws of cricket are hard, but they are clear. And like the laws of physics, their immutability is both beautiful and elegant. As a result, they encourage the aspirational quality of human nature. And inevitably, the intensity of cricket's lows magnifies the enjoyment of its highs. The fact that I do come back to cricket every time, no questions asked, week after week, surely says something about the quality of the game, and maybe, just maybe, something about the people who so love it.

So I do go out and umpire to complete my penance against Hambleden. Sure enough, my nemesis on the Hambleden team duly spills two easy catches ... aarrrghh!!

·5·

Declaration Cricket -
Noble Art or Magnificent Con?
Turville v. South Oxfordshire Amateurs,
Friday, 13 June, 2003

'If at first you don't succeed, try, try again. Then quit.
There's no use being a damn fool about it.'
W.C. Fields

I've tried. I really have. Much of this diary is concerned
with the timeless grace of cricket. But Declaration Cricket -
the formula whereby in village cricket the team batting first
voluntarily closes its innings, usually at tea time, to allow
their opponents an opportunity to bat - brings home for me
the importance of the contest. If the team batting second
fails to reach the target total, and the team bowling second
fails to take all 10 wickets, the match is drawn. I believe
that the heady mix that makes up cricket's appeal is under-
written by the need for a result. Forcing a draw, no matter
how stoutly the tenth and eleventh bats defend those last 10
overs, is just not a result (Shorter Oxford English
Dictionary, 'result = answer got by calculation' - *what's the
bloody answer!).*

In short, this polemic suggests that it's a confidence

trick, at least in village (and probably all amateur) forms of cricket. Declaration Cricket - more particularly, the ability to force 'draws' - has the potential, in my view, to undermine our faith in the game's seductive call. Contriving a match around the customs and traditions that are Declaration Cricket may be gracious, but so is Ballroom Dancing and, absent a six-a-side Knockout Tango Cup, or Claudia Schiffer as a weekly partner, you won't catch me spending six hours every Sunday on waltzes and foxtrots. I only keep playing Declaration Cricket because I want to change the system from the inside. This is a long range plan, you understand.

I am pleased to report that there is in fact a knock out village cricket competition. It is organised by *The Cricketer* magazine and has been running since 1972. This is a limited overs format of 40 overs per side, culminating in a final at Lords which can attract up to 8,000 people. Over 500 villages entered in 2003 (a village must not have any more than 3,000 people), including one of our traditional opponents, Britwell Salome. But one estimate suggests that there are 50,000 cricket clubs in England, with the more gentle 'Declaration' formula continuing to dominate at the village cricket level. And I am curious, why? After exhaustive research, I suspect the answer might be similar to the sophisticated response used to support the monarchy in this country (namely, *'Because'*).

Law 14 of the 2000 MCC Laws of Cricket states simply that 'the captain of the batting side may declare an innings closed … at any time during a match'. That's it. The rest is left up to custom and good conscience. For games that last up to five days, Law 14 is a sensible, even essential rule which adds a strategic dimension for captains. For amateur games which are compressed into a limited time span (i.e. one afternoon) the 'tradition' seems superfluous, even silly. Indeed, I have only ever seen two village games where the declaration has not been made right on the stroke of Afternoon Tea. In the first, against Woodcote, Turville declared 20 minutes before tea in order to have more time to get the opposing team out - a smart, but marginal, tactical decision (and seriously disruptive for Ruth, who was preparing the Afternoon Tea that day). In the second, against Ibstone, Turville batted on for three overs after tea against a very strong bowling team, in a forlorn attempt to build a defensible score. And this was regarded as being vaguely bad form.

In short, the 'strategic' use of declarations is effectively redundant in village cricket. The alternative is of course to allow each side a certain number of overs (say, 35) with the team achieving the highest total winning. This is entirely the basis for the development of Limited Overs cricket - which was successfully designed to win a new generation of supporters for the game.

Traditionalists will say, 'but Test matches allow for draws, and many of them have been very fine games'. Well, yes. But these are five day games, and a draw is often the outcome of an epic batting display, an epic demonstration of resistance, or an epic bout of English weather. There is nothing epic about the number nine and ten bats blocking out the last 10 overs of their 35 over innings in a typical village game, once they have decided that the target total is beyond them. And while I wouldn't go so far as to agitate for the removal of the 'draw' option from Test Match cricket (I'm pretty sure this would cause me difficulties with my immigration status in the UK), I'll bet there are many of us who have had slightly uncomfortable conversations with non-cricket loving friends (from America? Japan? France? the fairer sex?) which go something like this -

Friend: 'So, tell me more about this Test Cricket which you love so much. How long does it go for?'

You: 'Up to five days. (Three if either Australia or Zimbabwe are playing)'

Friend: (incredulous) 'Go on! It must be exciting?'

You: 'Well, over one third of all matches don't actually produce a winner'

Friend: 'YOU MUST BE MAD!! - you're sacked' (if you make the mistake of having this conversation with your boss from the New York head office)

Thank heavens you didn't have to rationalise any of the 'timeless' Test Matches that were prevalent in the first half of the 20th century. Like the Durban Test between England and South Africa in 1938, when England was set 696 to win in the last innings. After 10 (ten!) days, England had reached 654-3 before the match was abandoned to allow the Englishmen time to catch their boat back to England.

The other defence of Declaration Cricket is that it gives a captain more scope to involve players of varying abilities (e.g. bringing on a weaker bowler to tempt the opposition to ratchet up their run rate with some riskier strokes). This has some merit, but is still scarcely enough to justify colourless draws week after week. In any event, my experience in village cricket would suggest that the prevalence of batting collapses usually allows for regular batting opportunities for everyone. As for bowling, the quality of trundling is such that anyone who can land the ball in the batsman's half of the wicket with some regularity is likely to get more bowling than they would like.

There is of course the widespread belief that Declaration Cricket is a contributory factor to England's poor international cricket record in recent times. It is said by some critics to invite defensiveness and, as a consequence, fails to foster the winning attitude so prevalent in Australia, where Declaration Cricket sightings are rarer than those of the Minogue sisters. I don't actually buy this one. It's too simplistic. English cricket is simply going through the cyclical equivalent of Germany's economy. It will come good. I hope I'm right, otherwise the second hand BMW market could collapse.

Let me describe a typical example of Declaration Cricket, and let you decide if this is all just foaming at the mouth on my part. England, I shouldn't have to remind you, is the homeland of the great W.G. Grace, regarded by many informed judges as the father of the modern game, not only here in England, but also in Australia, the US and South Africa, countries where he led some of the first English cricket tours. No other player in the history of the game has, according to Henry Blofeld (in his 'Cricket And All That - An Irreverent History'), 'attracted so many stories which come under the heading of sharp practice ... he loved to win at more or less any cost'. Remember too, this is village cricket in a country which sired the father of modern economic thought, Adam Smith (well, Scotland sort of counts). If asked, Adam would I'm sure have said something like 'let the marketplace produce *results* that advance the common weal in the form of limited overs cricket' (I'm paraphrasing you understand). And don't get me started on Charles Darwin and Natural Selection.

I could have used any number of stultifying draws to make the case that Declaration Cricket is unhealthy. The local derby against Stonor, for example, saw three draws in three consecutive games in 2001 and 2002. In each case, these 'results' were ground out in the face of the team batting first having the clear upper hand (and fully deserving to win). With so much pride resting on these games, I don't understand how anyone can feel good about the outcome, and no one can believe for a minute that 'cricket is the winner'.

Our game against South Oxfordshire Amateurs, on the other hand, actually resulted in a win for SOA, but probably illustrates the point more completely. Contrived matches are anathema to 'real' cricket. On a warm mid-June afternoon (does it ever rain in this country?), we lost the toss and found ourselves in the field again. As ever, the pitch was flat, and the outfield fast, so it was a reasonable effort to keep the strong SOA combination to 223. In reply, Turville was quickly floundering at 20-3. This included two LBW's from the 167 year old SOA 'umpire' who I had made a special effort to cultivate a life long friendship with at the tea break. This failed so dismally that one of the LBW's was me. I was so far up the wicket at the time I was given out that I could shake hands with my batting partner, and enquire politely after the health of the umpire's seeing eye dog before storming off.

At this point, the South Oxfordshire captain took the recognised course and introduced some rubbish bowlers. This allowed Turville to belt lots of easy runs, and brought us to within 20 runs of the SOA total. Again, in line with accepted norms, the opposition skipper then brought back his two opening bowlers and strangled our run 'chase'. All of this was exactly as 'form' would prescribe, and SOA secured the last Turville wickets to emerge as worthy winners. But it was essentially a sham, and we laboured to this outcome for two hours longer than was strictly necessary. Two hours when we could have been down at the boozer grappling with knotty existential problems like 'Declaration Cricket: Noble Art or Magnificent Con?' or 'Alec Stewart, World Record Test Loser. Or What?'

Not only was the eventual result obtained farcically, but it could have been much worse. If Turville had somehow managed to pull off an unlikely victory, then we would have been completely unworthy winners. Equally, if Turville had managed to hold out for the last few overs for a draw to deny SOA its deserved win, then everyone would have been unhappy. Finally, even with SOA achieving its rightful win, I can't help feeling that the result was diminished by the ever so slightly humiliating way in which it was ultimately manufactured at our expense.

It's fine to lose. It's even acceptable to be beaten comprehensively (have I been in England for too long?). It is simply more important to have a real result. One you can either graciously boast about, or silently swear to avenge.

No one will remember the Turville v. South Oxfordshire Amateurs game in a month's time. This shouldn't necessarily lead to hyper-competitive League tables etc. On the other hand, at the end of the year it would be nice to look back and see that you have won more games than you have lost. The advent of 'Draws' makes any meaningful assessment of the 'success' of your season next to impossible. At the very least, a simple wins v. losses analysis would be an excuse for an extra couple of beers at the Annual General Meeting. Either that or some good natured teasing of the Captain.

Imagine an amateur village football match with an 8-0 half time scoreline. Is it even faintly conceivable that the stronger team would substitute a rubbish goalkeeper in order to produce a close result? Of course not. Is it likely that a rule might be introduced to say that there cannot be a winner until one team has scored 10 goals? (or whatever the football equivalent of taking ten wickets is). Ridiculous. It's not enough to say that this is exactly why cricket is 'noble' and therefore different. The charm and grace of cricket derives from the *manner* of its playing, not in the actual *outcome* of its playing. The outcome is key to the overall appeal of cricket, but only if the contest is genuine.

If teams are mismatched on a regular basis, then the fixture will simply become unenjoyable and should in time fade away. Much better than artificially sustaining it. I accept that there are fixtures like the one against South Oxfordshire Amateurs which have a long tradition, and should not be lightly discarded. For games in this category, the respective captains should be close enough to freely discuss team strength before the game, and *then* add the mystery Australian ring-in at the last moment. I'm sure W.G. would agree in principle ...

·6·

English Pubs
Turville v. Archery Tavern,
Saturday, 18 August, 2003

'Both parties repaired to the Swan Inn,
and spent the evening with the utmost hilarity and
good humour.'
**The Herts & Bucks Chronicle, on a match between
High Wycombe and Aylesbury (1827)**

It is of course impossible to talk about village cricket
in England, without entering one of that country's quaint,
idiosyncratic and cramped pubs. I entered many in the name
of research. The post-match ritual in England is identical to
Australia, and other countries around the world, with one
important exception. English pubs are barely big enough to
accommodate the five or six local denizens who visit on a
Saturday or Sunday evening. Squeezing in another 20 well
rounded and thirsty cricketers, who are at an age where they
have earned, and are used to receiving, generous personal
space, is a Houdini-like trick which every country pub
nevertheless seems to manage effortlessly.

Turville's local is the 'Fox and Hounds' at Christmas
Common, a village about three miles away from our
ground. The Fox & Hounds is a member of the Brakspears

group, which first began brewing beer in Henley in 1779, not very long after 'Terra Australis' was first introduced to England's peripatetic Captain Cook. This was enough for me to claim an instant affinity with the pub, although the mere act of walking into any English pub is usually sufficient to warrant my undying devotion. The choice of Turville's local watering hole is not a matter that is taken lightly. In fact, it was an official item of business at the 2002 Annual General Meeting. I know. I was there. The decision was perhaps not so surprising - the 'Fox & Hounds' management team's Power Point and flip chart presentation was so much better than the one put up by their competitors at 'The Crown'.

As a pub, the Fox & Hounds is traditional in every sense, except for a posh restaurant which has recently been added through the conversion of an adjoining barn. The only impact of this innovation on Turville's post match drinking has been to make parking even more reminiscent of a multi-car pile up on the M25 - cars are positioned at impossible angles in and alongside the hedgerows which line the narrow lane on which the pub sits.

The bar itself is well stocked with the local house bitter, Brakspears, as well as stuff you can actually drink, like Carlsberg, Stella Artois, Guinness and Hoegaarden - a fragrant Belgian beer that Jamie Hunt favours, but still sounds like the name of a Bavarian square dance to me.

As with English village names (see Chapter 14), this does offer me an opportunity to spend a moment poking fun at English beer names. Many of the more comical brands are associated with the Real Ale campaign (broadly non-keg beers). They include: 'Nettlethrasher', 'Skull-splitter' and 'Thrappledouser' (Roald Dahl characters, surely?), as well as 'Three Blind Mothers', 'Ale Mary' (oh, please), and my favourite, 'Dorothy Goodbodies Wholesome Stout'. I'm not surprised that Carlton & United Breweries decided that it was easier to 'Fosterise' the world than 'Dorothy Goodbodyise' it.

In any case, after a rather dispiriting loss against Archery Tavern, I find I am the first to arrive at the Fox & Hounds - some Australian traits are impossible to shake. (By the way, what is it with the English practice of faffing about for so long in the changing rooms after practice and after games? The relationship between an Englishman's appearance, and his careful attention to toilet and wardrobe remains perplexingly remote.) Shortly after my arrival, I am joined by Barnaby, and also Robert Gunn, our lethal left handed stand-and-deliver bat, and the second of our two Vice Captains.

Australian thirst quenching tends to organise itself along very efficient lines. Upon arriving at the bar, players arrange themselves into manageable groups ('schools') of up to five. With beer being served in seven ounce glasses, it is usually possible for each player to buy one round of drinks, and then to leave - merrily, but safely - after having consumed four or five modestly sized beers.

With Robert and Barnaby, I order three pints (lager for me - by now I am an established member of Turville, and no longer need to pander to the Brakspear bitter bores). In England, real men not only drink real ale, but they do it one pint at a time. That's a pint. Over half a litre, for the

49

metrically minded. Most of us think about these units of measurement only when we are buying milk for the family, or filling our cars with petrol. Other players soon begin to drift in, from both sides, and - remarkably - everyone manages to secure a drink, BUT WITHOUT ANY OBVIOUS SYSTEM. This is contrary to everything I have been taught about drinking etiquette ('Getting Legless The Australian Way'?).

By the end of the year, I'm sure the ad hoc manner of purchasing drinks evens out brilliantly amongst team mates, but for a nation which has invented such a complex game, with highly sophisticated rules (see Leg Before Wicket), how is it that the English can't be better organised with their drinking rituals?

I've been lucky enough to have been shoehorned into many wonderful pubs around the Oxfordshire countryside. But there is one in particular which I would plump for if it came to last drinks. For capturing most completely the quintessential English village cricket experience it is hard to go past (literally) the Six Bells at Warborough. The Warborough Cricket Club plays at the prettiest ground in all of Christendom. Sadly, the Turville v. Warborough fixture has now lapsed, as our rivals appear to be dedicated to more competitive fixtures. The Six Bells is a traditional, but otherwise unremarkable pub, except for the fact that it adorns the boundary line of this magical ground. Oh, and it is big enough to allow you to hold a pint and demonstrate that exquisite late cut you executed in the last over, without sending fellow patrons flying.

I first visited Warborough with Barnaby, who has been

unstinting in his support for my drinking 'field studies'. I must remind him to claim all those pints as a tax deduction. We had in fact played a match that day not for Turville, but rather for the South Oxfordshire Amateurs. Martin Fennell had inveigled Barnaby and me to play in this fixture. Martin was a regular for the South Oxfordshire Amateurs, as well as our rivals, Stonor. He also turned out consistently for Turville. And a local club team in Cape Town. His diary (if not his marriage) must be a complete mess. We played this day at Radley Boys College, a posh public (Australia 'private', more widely 'pots of money') school in Oxfordshire. Warborough, and the Six Bells, was on the way home (honest, Felicity!).

It is worth a brief digression on the Radley game. The South Oxfordshire Amateurs, whom we have met already, are what is known as a 'wandering' side, with no home ground (and therefore no mouldy nets, or cranky curators). The playing complement of SOA was comprised of people like Martin Fennell, and other cricket 'tragics' who needed (and could manage) a mid-week cricket fix. Interestingly, with the collapse in equity markets around the world, there was a healthy number of former City bankers and brokers supplementing the SOA player list in the Summer of 2003. The game against the Radley First XI took place on the school's main playing field. It was a belter of a pitch - one of the TWO HUNDRED strips which the school maintains, on what is reputedly the largest mown surface in England. As if this wasn't enough, we were playing next to the school's carefully manicured nine hole golf course.

The match itself was unmemorable (alright, we were

stuffed comprehensively by the school boys), but the public school thing was eye-opening. At tea, for example, and also after the game, the Radley boys (who incidentally all wear gowns during the day for lessons) immediately donned their Navy Blue Sports Blazers in order to entertain their guests. At my age, and with my experience, I was surprised to find that this was strangely intimidating. I instantly had a better appreciation of the psychological impact of the Australian Test Team all wearing their Baggy Green caps in the first session of every Test Match.

In the charming Club House after the Radley game, Barnaby and I have some fun looking for a photo of a current Turville team mate who was once a Radley student. Pictures of every Radley First XI from the late 19th century adorn the walls, and we finally discover dear old Clive ('Clive Charles Wathen Seigal') in the 1966 shot, proudly sporting the very naff silk cravat (with aforementioned Navy Blazer) that each boy must wear to become part of this piece of the school's history.

As part of my responsibilities as Turville's Australian conscience, I have been gently introducing my team mates to the art of slagging each other off. This is not something which comes naturally to Englishmen in genteel village cricket. For Australians however, the ribbing of team mates represents about 67 per cent of the total enjoyment which we derive from the game.

The silk cravat episode allowed me to crank up my education, with Clive as the unsuspecting target. Naturally, CCW Seigal, Esq. remained majestically above the taunting, pointing out that he rather thought the Radley garb flattered both he and Ted Dexter (another Radley old boy, and subsequently English Test Captain).

Happily, the South Oxfordshire Amateur hacks have the last laugh at Radley. After our drubbing, the School graciously opened up the bar, and the beer tasted just a little bit sweeter for watching the lads gagging for the drink which their Masters could never permit.

Meanwhile, back at the Fox & Hounds, we are busy exaggerating our rather sorry efforts in the Archery Tavern match, including Barnaby's prodigious attack on the scones at afternoon tea (and his equally prodigious, if intermittent, intestinal attacks on the fresh country air during our turn in the field). My achievement in taking the only opposition wicket to fall has been transmogrified into 'Wade snared 100 per cent of the wickets'. I decide to leave the pub having consumed two pints, not long after we declare ourselves 'moral victors' on the day. Two pints is already about 15% more refreshment than five beers in my Australian 'school'. It's a good thing British motorways are reasonably uncluttered at 10 o'clock on Sunday evenings ...

Cricket Tragics

Turville v. Invalids, Saturday, 14 June, 2003

'They say I wasted my money. I say 90% went on women, fast cars and booze. The rest I wasted.'
George Best

Like any self-respecting addict in denial, I would of course strenuously reject any suggestion that I am a 'cricket tragic'. As proof, I tender the evidence of a dinner which I enjoyed with Steve Waugh and his Manager in Madras in early 2002 (Steve was the PR face of a life insurance business I was launching in India). To the best of my recollection, I didn't drool. I didn't even come away with an autograph.

The hero worship of Steve in India was extraordinary, but I didn't really blame Steve's Manager too much for his fawning. The Indians were also overawed. It certainly made my job much easier. At the Press Conference following the launch, there were no pesky questions about how we expected to get our brand new insurance business known in India. The rows and rows of press in attendance, followed by the wall to wall media coverage the next morning, made this concern redundant. I was also prepared to respond to tricky questions about how we would compete against the big State owned insurance companies. No problem. All the assembled throng wanted to know was how Steve felt about being left out of the Australian One Day side.

I asked if Steve could join me for my regular Presentations to the Board back in Australia. I even promised not to do that 'between us we have made over 10,000 Test runs', gag any more. He looked at me with that knowing half grin of his, but was gracious enough not to use the 'Tragic' word. After spending three days with Steve, he turned out to be completely true to label. Determined, business like, reliable, although perhaps just a little grim. And that was just checking out of the hotel. He was a perfect ambassador for a life and health insurance business, although when we both went down with illnesses in Bombay, I was a little anxious about the prospect of testing the quality of our product.

There have been other occasions when I have been more worried about slipping into Tragic-ville. Perhaps the worst instance was when my ancient and trusty Gray Nicholls bat disintegrated in one of the Derby Games against Stonor. Once I had emerged from therapy, I was desperate for a replacement weapon. Three other Turville players had found a chap who had tailor made bats for them in the previous season. They looked spanking to me, so I rang 'The Handmade Bat Company' (no, really), and said 'I'll have one the same as Barnaby's'. I paid over the odds for a rush job, but the real drama came when we had to arrange delivery.

On the Saturday morning of my next game, I rang and offered to go out to Newbury to collect the bat. My saviour actually responded that he would be happy to drive to a convenient mid-point in order to save me some time. This is why the English service industry is renowned around the world (?). Unfortunately, *I* was new to the country, and *he* didn't have much of an idea where I was living. In the end, we settled on a liaison on the M4 off- ramp to Heathrow airport. And so, with traffic whizzing by, and jet engines drowning out our conversation, we completed our transaction from the boot of his Mercedes in the emergency lane. The urgency, and the setting, made me feel rather like I was pulling off a major drug deal. After, we shook hands and rather sheepishly returned to our cars before pulling back into the traffic.

'Cricket tragics' are like elephants - difficult to describe, but you know one when you see one. All teams have one or more, and they are always regarded with affection (and perhaps just the tiniest amount of pity - 'there but for the grace of god, etc'). My favourite definition of a cricket tragic is someone who, on a Job Application form, under the question 'Greatest Disappointment' writes 'Graeme Hick's Test Career'. But they come in many different shapes and sizes - inveterate Committee animals who seem to live at the Club, Wisden wielding ancients who never miss a day at Lords (even against Zimbabwe), grown men who cried over Phil Tufnell's last Tour Diary, and businessmen who can't get enough of the Sponsors Tent, at cricket charity matches featuring minor cricket celebrities.

All this is helpful background to the traditional Turville fixture against Invalids and in turn to one of our resident cricket tragics, Simon Stracey. Simon is genial, passionate, and a magnificent member of the Turville Park Cricket Club. If nothing else, he deserves a Life Membership for recruiting Jamie Hunt to the Club all those years ago. Intriguingly, however, for someone who has chosen cricket as their preferred form of weekend relaxation, Simon cannot bat, is reluctant to bowl, runs between wickets a little like the Sugar Plum Fairy, and is still coming to grips with the task of simultaneously bending over to the ground and arresting the progress of a moving cricket ball. He does however possess massive hands, which allow him to pull off at least one outrageous catch every season.

Simon was Match Manager for the Invalids game, which meant that he had the normal responsibilities of marshalling a side, organising Afternoon Tea, and ringing us all up at mid-day when the match was called off due to the rain. Happily for Simon (who would otherwise have been eating sponge cake for a week), and for us, the rain stayed away for the Invalids game. In fact, the weather was spectacular. Warm (about 25 degrees), bright blue skies, and a gentle breeze to protect us from overheating. A children's birthday party taking place at Lord Sainsbury's Manor House next door meant that there were a large number of fathers sneaking out at regular intervals to look longingly at our contest.

The Invalids team was another wandering side like South Oxfordshire Amateurs, and traced its roots back to The Great War. Returning servicemen banded together to begin the great tradition of this eclectic side which, given its history, appeared to attract a greater per capita share of cricket tragics. I was particularly impressed by the Invalids' blazers and caps, decorated by horizontal stripes of lurid gold and powder blue. I mean, how did that idea get launched at Committee level? The colours are in fact from the hospital's army officer's wartime pyjamas (what else?), but the design is particularly ostentatious. Packer's one-day cricket revolution, and its 'colour pyjamas', was tame compared to this lot.

The Turville v. Invalids game is not terribly far removed from Archie Macdonell's fictionalised 1930's account of a village cricket game between Invalids, and the Kentish village of Fordenden ('England, Their England'). This story is the one with the famously compelling three page description of the catch taken by the Invalids 'ring-in' American, to secure the most unlikely of ties ('At last the ball came down. To Mr. Hodge it seemed a long time before the invention of Sir Isaac Newton finally triumphed'). It also tells of the mayhem caused by the Invalids' Mr. Harcourt upon mischievously no-balling the menacing village black-smith. This caused Harcourt (a poet, naturally) to conclude that he 'did not think the world had ever been, or could ever be again, quite such a capital place'.

The playing complement for the Invalids over the years had included Boris Karloff, Evelyn Waugh, Godfrey Evans, Tony Hancock and Turville's own cravat connoisseur, Clive Seigal (currently the Invalids 'Dinner Secretary'), along with the upright John Leefe. While Turville cannot quite live up to such an illustrious player list, it does boast a number of other characters with claims to cricket tragic status. There is of course Barnaby, who on reading an early proof of this work declared (with total sincerity) that he had never really thought of himself as an eccentric (!). This obviously suggests that Barnaby has a view of 'normality' which would appeal to Inspector Clouseau. Neil Runkel is Turville's deceptive spin bowler (in that he actually spins the ball). He wears a sweater in 30 degree heat, and talks endlessly about the game in a style which suggests he has left his monocle at his City Club. Then there is Toby Greenwood who, as a cricketer, makes a very fine country solicitor, but an even better commentator on his special category (everything). Other characters include John Hancock, our opening bat, groundsman and professional *agent provocateur,* and Ollie Brett, the intense BBC sports writer and local aristocrat, who fields every innocuous forward defensive prod which happens in his direction as if he were Jonty Rhodes, frantically attempting to run out Steve Waugh.

There are also the anti-eccentrics, who are all as 'tragic' in their own way. These are the people without whose diligence and hard work we could have ten minute AGM's. For Turville, this includes Mike Wicks, one of the Club's elder statesmen, fixture secretary and all-round fixer. Mike tells of his recruitment into the Turville Park Cricket Club fold on the day he moved to Turville in 1975. Seeing the removal van installing the family Wicks, Air Chief Vice Marshall Sir Christopher Foxlee-Norris (no less) press-ganged Mike into service that same day. He confirmed this kerb side conscription with a note shortly after which began 'Dear Wicks' (you don't find this kind of warmth in just any old club). John Leefe is a ramrod straight character who, amongst other things, works tirelessly on producing quality pitches week after week. John shares these responsibilities with John Hancock, but bizarrely they work almost entirely independently of each other. Communication between the two is often through intermediaries. If they ever bat together, the running between wickets is an object lesson in brooding silence. Then there is Club Secretary, David Cairns, who in his spare time has been awarded an OBE for services to accounting (until you have a chance to meet David, you will have to content yourself with his 1999 pot-boiler 'Applying International Accounting Standards'). The balance of the membership is comprised of a healthy cross section of professionals, farmers, students, businessmen, and others who are gainfully employed, and therefore unlikely to find the time needed to instruct solicitors in order to challenge the defamatory things I am writing about them.

The game against Invalids itself was played in impeccable spirit and style, and our guests secured a ten run victory after nearly 400 runs were scored during the course of the afternoon. Invalids were helped by a Cambridge 'Blue' who scored 80 and finished off Turville's run chase with a hat trick. This was not as the script should have unfolded. Archie Macdonell's Invalids also sported a Cambridge Blue back in the 1930's - a giant who was 'called, simply, Boone'. It was only after a first ball duck that Boone was revealed to have secured his blue at Cambridge for Rowing rather than Cricket. Maybe we should have set Barnaby (Boxing Blue) onto the Invalids Blue this day at Turville.

The truth is, we are probably all slightly 'tragic' in our own way for pursuing our recreation through the medium of cricket. For me, however, the afternoon of the Invalids game showed once again that the level of tragedy reaches its peak in this country when the sun comes out, however briefly, and otherwise respectable Englishmen (like Simon Stracey) feel compelled to expose their skinny white torsos to the world. There should be a law ...

· 8 ·

Captaincy

Turville v. Brightwell cum Sotwell,
Sunday, 29 June, 2003

'The secret of life is honesty and fair dealing.
If you can fake that, you've got it made'
Groucho Marx

I have a confession to make. Captaincy is not actually hard to 'do'. It is certainly tough being the team's figure-head when things aren't working out, but the 'doing' itself requires not much more than the ability to keep your head, look stern and thoughtful as often as possible (simultaneously is good), and keep count of your bowler's overs. This is the dirty little secret of the cricket captain's fraternity. I expect I will receive a Notice of Excommunication from the doyen of captains, Mike Brearley, whose 1985 tome 'The Art of Captaincy' takes 296 pages to recognise (but not actually say) 'it was Botham wot won it'.

Test Cricket's most successful Captain, Steve Waugh, has committed his secrets to a series of Tour Diaries. These reveal an extraordinarily single minded focus on winning every session of every match. They also show a captain who cleverly balances the need to bond with his team mates, whilst maintaining his authority. This is not as easy as it sounds. But otherwise, captaincy seems to come down to instinct and luck.

Maybe I've been lucky too. I have captained sides in Australia, Singapore and England. All teams were successful, and we participated in Finals cricket where this was possible. This is largely because my personnel were grown ups, who didn't require much hand holding. Not even the fast bowlers. Interestingly, my most successful side was the Singapore Cricket Club team, where we won the League Title, the Knockout Cup and the Play Off finals in a single season. The core of this side was made up of five Englishmen, two Australians, an Indian (from the South), an Indian (from the North), three Singaporeans of Indian extraction, one of Pakistani extraction, and an Icelander. I made that last one up, but there might just as well have been, for all the notice that was taken of the many different backgrounds.

So, with this modicum of experience, I have made a point of analysing the different styles of captaincy which prevail on the village cricket circuit. For convenience, I have managed to reduce my analysis to three major styles -

⊖ the 'What Time is Afternoon Tea' group (31 per cent)
⊖ the 'It's A Noble Game' group (62 per cent), and
⊖ the 'Win At All Costs' group (7 per cent)

Naturally, I make no apologies for the outrageously over-simplified, and totally unscientific conclusions which follow.

What Time is Afternoon Tea?

The typical 'Afternoon Tea' captain is 55, portly and gregarious. The social occasion is the main reason for turning out, and the cricket is usually secondary - sometimes even a nuisance. While quaint in its own way, these games are to be avoided. The underpinning reason for lavishing so much time and affection on the game must surely be to come together as a team for the purpose of achieving something, both individually, and as a team. Something more than gorging on cream cakes anyway.

As a result of this captain's singular focus, the pitch is usually woefully under-prepared, the game starts 40 minutes late, Tea is called early, and the second innings is dispensed with rapidly in order to get to the pub as quickly as possible. These captains often waste a lot of time making senseless adjustments to the field to remind everyone that they are in fact captain. At our level, batsmen are unable to place their shots to within 30 metres. It is therefore the height of absurdity when our 'Afternoon Tea' captain moves his fieldsmen three metres to the left at deep backward square leg. The net result of all of this is often a 20 over game which takes up the whole day. Eighty runs is typically a winning total. Cricket is not so romantic that this can be regarded in any sense as worthwhile.

'Afternoon Tea' captains do not exist in Australia. Probably either shot or deported. Either that or they just died out through natural selection, given how rubbish Australian Afternoon Teas are.

It's A Noble Game

These are my favourites. The 'Noble Game' captains genuinely believe that matches must be played in the right spirit to ensure that 'Cricket is the Winner'. As if there really is some heavenly being keeping a running tally: 'Oh, there's another bonus point for Cricket, which puts it way ahead of Golf this month, but still just slightly behind Lawn Bowls'.

'Noble Game' captains are focussed on giving all of their players a fair turn at batting or bowling, and of course especially concerned about engineering a close game. (Most 'Noble Game' captains are not so noble that they will concede a win to the opposing team if a draw can be secured.) Nevertheless, making all of the above conditions come together in a way which achieves the right outcome/s is possibly the most difficult captaincy there is. Sort of like managing a professional law or accounting partnership in a way that allows all your partners to be successful, at the same time as guaranteeing the success of your clients, and also the profession. Oh, wait, that's the way it's supposed to work, isn't it. But the 'Noble Game' captain at least has to do it outside, exposed to England's fickle weather. I have enormous admiration for captains who regularly and successfully manage their resources and their matches according to the 'Noble Game' philosophy.

Mostly, 'Noble Game' captains are talented, and have enjoyed a successful cricket career. This means they are secure with themselves, and conscious of the debt which they owe to the game. More than anything, I like playing against teams led by 'Noble Game' captains because we can stuff them out of sight.

Win At All Costs

Mercifully, only seven per cent of village cricket captains are of the 'Win At All Costs' genus. Either born in Australia, or with relatives out there, they are typically never older than 30, and almost always sport a chip on both shoulders. Even tossing the coin before the match can be a desperate and combative event for the 'Win At All Costs' captain.

I do actually struggle to understand these guys. The attitude is fine, but the forum is totally inappropriate for its expression. It's a bit like having Gordon Ramsay come out from Claridges to cater for our afternoon teas. Winning is a laudable ambition, but not by bowling your two openers unchanged for 40 overs.

In the main, 'Win At All Costs' captains have yet to grasp the subtlety and charm which should attend Sunday afternoon declaration cricket. It could happen in time, but my experience would suggest that these 'Angry Young Men' eventually become 'Grumpy Middle Aged Tosspots', and ultimately 'Lonely Old Geezers'. And failed captains.

●

Naturally, I have had an opportunity to study Turville's captain, Paul Girdler, in some detail. Paul has always struck me as a little like Ethelred the Unready, never quite sure about imposing himself on his team, or on a game. He is a useful medium fast opening bowler who can also turn his hand to spin if needed, but tends to overbowl himself and our other main bowlers. In large part, this is because our bowling resources are fairly thin, but variety is both courageous and fun. When a bowling change works, captains typically receive a puzzling share of the credit. When it doesn't work, you either blame the bowler, or try to pass the decision off as 'imaginative' captaincy. Paul also has a predisposition to bowl first, but then he shares this trait with lots of English Test captains. In part this is a function of the format (Declaration Cricket) which means that batting second you can win, but should never lose (i.e. you can always grind out a draw if in difficulty).

Perhaps most importantly though, for a relatively tender 28 year old, Paul does 'get' village cricket. He cleverly affects a 'Noble Game' persona, while still secretly harbouring just enough of the 'Win At All Costs' approach to ensure that Turville wins more games than it loses. For even more gravitas, I have suggested that Paul should grow a beard and stroke it - much as Mike Gatting was fond of doing. No one believed for a minute that Gatting was thinking of anything other than the barmaid down at the local pub, but at least he looked like he really wanted to Win *Something* At All Costs.

Against Brightwell cum Sotwell, Paul wins the toss AND BATS! Just as we are thinking that perhaps we need to reassess his captaincy, Paul makes the mistake of confessing that he has just enjoyed a big lunch at the local pub, having played nine holes of golf beforehand. He quietly slopes off for a gentle snooze as he sends his bats out to do battle. However it was arrived at, the decision turns out to be an inspired one, and Turville compiles a very handy 269. Robert Gunn crunched 68 not out (with only three singles!), and Jamie laid about the attack for a powerful 66. I got 105, and had a very nice time, thank you for asking.

Frustratingly, we are only able to secure nine of the necessary ten wickets by the time the game finishes just before 8.00pm. Brightwell cum Sotwell never threatened our total, finishing on 142. Paul has done everything right today, cleverly rotating his bowlers, serving up plenty of slow stuff, and even taking five wickets himself with some well flighted off spin. But then he lets himself down by describing the outcome as 'a good day out'. That may be, but it is still strangely deflating to end on a note where the clearly inferior opposition feel like the victors for having prevented a well deserved Turville win. It is also strangely at odds with Paul's passionate support for the English Cricket Team to win at every outing.

The opposition captain is clearly a 'Noble Game' man. His eyes are misted over at the Dunkirk-like spirit exhibited by his numbers 10 and 11 bats in defying the Turville invaders on his pitch. Oh well, at least we can rely on the skipper to ply us with beer to celebrate his five wicket haul … Paul, Paul? … where has Paul gone? ... Oh bugger, that just leaves me ...

·9·

Leg before Wicket - Scourge of the Modern Game

Turville v. Harpsden, Sunday, 16 September, 2001

'If the game cannot get its decisions right, it deserves to become a laughing stock.'

Henry Blofeld

Although I am primarily a batsman, I do understand the genesis of the Leg Before Wicket rule, so I want to tackle the application of the rule in modern day cricket in a calm and rational manner. It sucks and I hate it.

At Harpsden, we were facing a very sharp-ish attack as we chased a respectable total of 190 on a variable wicket. At 35-3, and after a run of poor innings, I had my chance to grab the game by the scruff of the neck, get Turville's (and my) season back on track, and trot out many more of the Wisden approved metaphors which are mandatory in accounts of this nature. After some nervous moments, I felt like I was beginning to get a handle on the attack. At this point I was idly aware of an umpiring change which brought team mate Colin Simon out to officiate. Colin is a very good opening bat, a lovely man, and (warning bells) scrupulously fair. This is no doubt handy as an accountant, and also as the Club Treasurer, but should have had absolutely no place in the course of entertaining the LBW appeal which was made against me in the very next over. Now one of my great advantages in these situations is that I am a relatively untidy batsman, and tend to shuffle about my crease a lot. This, combined with the meaningful stare which I offered Colin, should have been enough in this case for him to study the appeal thoughtfully (he did), and firmly turn the appeal down (he didn't). My meaningful stare turned into a most un-gentlemanly glare, and I trooped off. There is a good chance I was in fact out, but - as with so many LBW dismissals - it would have required a slow motion replay, a theodolite, and 30 minutes of trigonometric calculations to be absolutely certain.

In the amateur form of the game, there is no place for such a complicated and subjective rule, administered by individuals who have no business stuffing up my Sunday afternoon. In my career, I have seen applications of the LBW Law that have been capricious, wrong-headed, inept, arbitrary and obscene. And that was just Colin's decision. I can confidently say that LBW appeals and decisions have given rise to more than half of the 'bad blood' which I have witnessed in cricket. In village cricket, the English are much more relaxed about awarding LBW decisions against their own team mates. This over developed sense of doing the right thing by the game would see them come to extreme physical harm were they to apply this approach in the Melbourne South Suburban League. I would like to think that this is not so much that Australians are necessarily less 'fair', but more that they have a keener appreciation of the inherent 'unfairness' of the LBW law. I would like to think this, but it would of course be bollocks.

At the professional level, I concede that the issue is more complicated when we are discussing people's livelihoods. The distribution of LBW decisions in International cricket makes a particularly fascinating case study. Only three bowlers in history have taken more than 100 LBW wickets. Wasim Akram - 119 (28 per cent of total wickets taken); Kapil Dev - 110 (25 per cent) and Waqar Younis - 110 (29 per cent). Then comes Shane Warne - 95 (19 per cent) and Sir Richard Hadlee - 83 (19 per cent). The difference between one LBW decision in less than four wickets (for the great fast bowlers who ply their trade largely on the sub-continent) and one in more than five wickets (for the rest) is hard to dismiss as a statistical aberration.

And of course the advent of modern technology (notably 'Hawkeye') proves how often LBW decisions are just plain wrong. Even Hawkeye is far from failsafe - it can't possibly account completely accurately for the impact of variable bounce. Hawkeye itself claims that, of 21 LBW's awarded in English Test cricket in Season 2002, its technology showed only 13 of them heading for the stumps. That's a 62 per cent pass rate, barely a 'C'. Too many umpires are patently framing their decisions on the 'Balance of Probabilities'. Imagine an umpire saying to a batsman, who has just played and missed, 'Oh, that was a corker of a ball ... I'm giving you out because you played a 'C' shot at it, and obviously weren't even good enough to get the snick on it which it deserved'. Maybe this is just another manifestation of the 'grade inflation' which is afflicting British life?

If this is going on in First Class cricket, you can guess the margin (chasm?) of error in village and park cricket. I think of LBW in the same way people think of jury trials (eh ...?). Better that the system works in a way that allows 100 'guilty' men to go free, rather than sending one 'innocent' man to jail (or back to the pavilion, if you follow my drift). Remember too, the formal manifestation of cricket's guidelines are quite deliberately framed as Laws. Not rules. Not regulations. Not policies. Surely, it's only right in these circumstances that we interpret these Laws using the highest possible standards. I'm pretty certain Lord Denning would agree. In short, it's time that the traditional cricket custom of awarding batsmen 'the benefit of the doubt' received, well, 'the benefit of the doubt'.

Now, for those batsmen who are still with me (I assume I lost any bowlers who actually read the Chapter heading), I even have a solution. Let's re-formulate Leg Before Wicket as 'Wilful or Careless Obstruction.' I know, I know, this introduces another layer of subjectivity, namely - 'What was the batsman thinking about with that ridiculously striped cap?' But surely, umpires are capable of assessing when batsmen are deliberately getting in the way? For example, when they offer no shot, or take guard outside off stump, or arrive at the crease with their football boots on. It is not an original thought of course. This is essentially how the LBW law was first framed in 1774, although '*deliberate* obstruction' was removed by the MCC as a condition for an LBW dismissal soon after, in 1787. Henry Blofeld, in his 'Cricket And All That - An Irreverent History', suggests that the decision in 1787 was reached 'with the help of a glass or two of black velvet'. Even so, the 1809 Code, at Law 20, continued to imply some 'intent' when it spoke of a batsman who '... *with his foot or leg he stops the ball'*. It is of course also notable that the over arm bowling action had not yet arrived, and the LBW law was probably tightened to inhibit batsmen, who were clearly enjoying the upper hand at this time. Indeed, it was not until the 1820s that over arm bowling first began to become acceptable, and this was in large part due to the bigger and bigger totals teams were running up.

If nothing else, my suggested re-interpretation might at least encourage umpires to limit their judgements to only those appeals where a batsman is behind the popping crease, squared up, bat nowhere in sight, and hit on the ankle in front of middle stump (not off stump, and not leg stump). The technical definition of this remarkable concatenation of events is 'Out'. If you think I'm over-larding it, here is a quick reminder of the key terms of the LBW Law, taken from the 2000 MCC Code -

Law 36 - *a batsmen is out LBW where, '... the point of impact ... is between wicket and wicket and ... (e) but for the interception, [the ball] would have hit the wicket ...'*

That's 'WOULD HAVE', not *might* have, or *could* have, or *should* have. And certainly not 'Oh you've appealed A LOT, and so it must be in the vicinity'. This is the umpire that really gets my goat, the one who simply gets worn down by appeals. It reminds me of one of my more difficult bowlers in Singapore. When I asked him once why he had appealed for a rather frivolous LBW (which was in fact given out) he replied, of the departing batsman, 'well he missed it, didn't he?'

But at least in village cricket we don't usually have to put up with umpires who are paid to officiate. This is of course common in many Grade and competition cricket leagues around the world. In the main, this group is represented by individuals who believe that they are being paid to 'do stuff'. They are therefore predisposed to make decisions (invariably marginal, and therefore dodgy ones) on the basis that this offers us all more 'value' for our umpiring dollar. I confess I did encounter one such specimen at Turville. He awarded eight LBWs in our game (on my count, this was roughly four in five appeals!). A dear old soul, but I fear the biggest mistake we made in that game was thrusting our pads so far down the pitch that we brought ourselves within this umpire's field of vision. We should have just stayed back out of harms way.

Maybe I should just stop shuffling in front of my stumps? No ... complaining about it is much more fun. And so, after I trudge off at Harpsden, my team mates offer me the statutory condolences - 'that looked high? wide? handsome?' This makes my rapprochement with Colin slightly strained when he comes off to explain his decision - 'It was out'. When next you are batting Colin, watch out if you see me donning the White Umpire's Coat. I checked, Law 36 says nothing about umpires appealing for LBW's themselves ...

·10·

Touring
Turville in France, 13-16 July, 2001

'First the hunter, the missionary and the
merchant, next the soldier and the politician, and
then the cricketer -
that is the history of British civilisation.
And of these civilizing influences the last may,
perhaps, be said to do the least harm.'
Cecil Headlam

One of the singular pleasures of amateur cricket is
offered by the opportunity to travel, and to share your
strange passion not only with team mates, but also with
other like minded citizens of the world. Playing in
Singapore allowed me to indulge this pleasure almost
every week, as we were either on tour, or entertaining
teams on their way to or from England, Australia or the
sub-continent. For village cricket teams, the opportunities
for travel are much more limited; however, in 2001, I found
myself on tour with Turville in France.

Most readers will appreciate that France is not one of the
cricket world powers, even though it wields a veto on the
UN Security Council, and might therefore one day decide

that it is, in fact, World Champion. From time to time stories do actually surface in which the French claim to have introduced the game of cricket into England in the 1300s. This claim is patently false, as even the most casual reference to the modest quality of English Afternoon Teas will demonstrate.

Our Tour Leader for this French adventure was none other than the indefatigable Barnaby, and the arrangements fell into place in the same unique way that Barney kept wicket, namely, with a minimum of style and forethought but (miraculously) effective results. The official Tour Party numbered twenty, of which the Wade Family made up *eight* (Ruth, me, our four children - Georgia, Thomas, Harriet and Prudence, who all promised to marry badly if they weren't mentioned in these diaries - and Ruth's parents, Bob and Joan, who were on their annual pilgrimage from Melbourne for the Northern Summer). The fact that we were 40 per cent of the total touring group showed my commitment to the Turville cause, and Ruth's commitment to 'share' her parents with me.

The Wade Travelling Circus had in fact managed a week of pre-tour sightseeing in Normandy and the Loire Valley (Tour Option 'B', in the 56 page Tour Brochure) before joining up with the other 60 per cent of our party in Brittany, at a very well equipped resort called Domaines des Ormes. The resort was made up of a hotel, serviced apartments, a camping ground, an 18 hole golf course, a lake for water sports, a stream for fishing, and a massive swimming pool and childrens games complex. Oh, and a cricket ground. It was perfect.

But ever so slightly surreal. Over the four days of our stay, we were to play in a triangular competition against the local French team, Les Ormes, and our traditional Channel Islands rivals, The Jersey Farmers, who had also trekked down to Brittany for the long weekend. The cricket pitch was artificial, but the field and surrounds were very real and very lush, and all of it was set in the shadow of a striking 17th century Chateau standing guard at deep fine leg ('... and here comes John Leefe from the Louis XVI end ...'?).

As this was mid-way through my first season with Turville, there were still some Club Members who I hadn't met. Unfortunately for Guy Peppiatt, the team bookie, I was a complete stranger. We arrived at Domaine des Ormes on Friday, just in time to see Guy completing the book on Turville's expected highest run scorer and wicket taker. I noticed Paul, the skipper, wearing a self satisfied grin but thought nothing else of it. He was in love, after all.

Our first match was against Jersey on Saturday. Turville would be defending the Jersey Ashes which was contested each year, alternating between Henley and St. Helier. The weather had been grim for two days, but we were keen to get the 'I played cricket in France' T-shirts (well who wouldn't be), so the briefest respite in the rain allowed us to make a start. Turville lost the toss, and the Jersey skipper said *apres-vous*. As it happened, the conditions improved dramatically, and we rattled up 311 (not a typo) in 40 overs. I managed 120 and, as a result, Paul cleaned out Guy Peppiatt, having made a big plunge on me as highest run getter at odds of 20-1. So much for Marquis of Queensbury.

In Paul's defence, we were in France, so different standards might have been said to apply.

And so I had achieved every schoolboy cricketer's dream - 100 in France(?). It almost matched my other career 'highlight'- being capped for my country, Singapore (?!). (In 1990, when residency qualifications were notoriously lax). Back in France, my children were in the swimming pool, and singularly unimpressed when they heard. Bob, my father-in-law, and an old cricket war horse from the days of 'six o'clock closing' in Melbourne pubs (which resulted in lots of five-thirty declarations), was my only family supporter. Even he thought I played across the line too much.

Jersey began their rather forlorn chase just as the weather began to close in again. To their great credit they soldiered on, and even threatened momentarily, when their key bat smashed a quick fire 75. But with his departure, Jersey's 'French resistance' crumbled, and they fell for 225 to rousing cheers of 'Vive la Turville' and - for no particular reason - 'Down with the Frogs' (old habits die very hard it would seem). For the sake of team unity I was compelled to join in. Well, they did sink the Greenpeace boat, the 'Rainbow Warrior' in New Zealand.

That night, we enjoyed a brilliant meal, produced effortlessly for we *rosbifs* by the otherwise unprepossessing hotel restaurant. This was followed by some typically awful speechifying. When you are part of a group sharing a special interest like cricket, speeches are almost always a no-lose occasion. Either they are very good (rare), and the rewards for the listener are obvious. Or they are awful (commonplace), and the fun lies in the obvious embarrassment caused to a team mate. Bizarrely, people not part of the group can find this tiresome and unfunny. Go figure.

Touring is also an interesting phenomenon in the way it strips away inhibitions. Reserved Englishmen who are ordinarily cagey ('go on, tell me your first name, please Mr. Leefe ...?'), become much more gregarious and, well, friendly. Strange race. It's a lot like the English expatriate crowd in Singapore who were genuine 'heart on the sleeve' patriots, blubbering over the Windsors at the first sign of an approaching St. Georges Day, or Night At The Proms celebration. Back home, of course, they lampoon the Royals on a healthily routine basis.

The next day was devoted to sightseeing (or recovering, for those who had ignored the skipper's strict 3am curfew) and golf. Domaine des Ormes was brilliantly positioned about 30 miles away from, respectively, Mont St. Michel, Dinan and St-Malo. The Wades hiked up to Mont St. Michel to gawp at the magnificent island of Mont Tombe, crowned by an 11th century Abbey, and protected by tides moving at speeds of up to 10 km per hour (slightly quicker than our 'spinner', Ollie Brett, was launching his donkey drops against Jersey). The rather tacky tourist shops, and the return of the wet weather could not detract from this jaw dropping sight, said to be the real inspiration for the Disneyland castle in Fantasyland. Don't wait for a Cricket World Cup in France. See it now.

A leisurely round of golf in the afternoon, followed by dinner in the spectacular medieval town of Dinan, with its Gothic bridges and cobblestoned market avenues, was enough on its own to justify the bloody awful ferry trip that is needed to get from England to the Continent and back. Our final round of local sightseeing took us to St-Malo the following morning to see this striking walled city on the Brittany coastline. The imposing ramparts, cobbled streets, and 18th century buildings, when combined with the sunshine, the food, the pervasive sense of history (St-Malo was heavily bombed in WW2), and the overall French attitude of 'stuff you' (to everything, not just tourists), made this a very intoxicating place to visit.

Next up in our triangular series came the local team, Les Ormes. Not so much the 'Flower of French Youth', as the 'Essence of English Antiquity', Les Ormes was made up largely of refugees from English weather, English food, English beer and the NHS. We nevertheless contrived to lose this game, with the opposition enjoying the home ground advantage, a lucky toss, some fortunate umpiring decisions (did I leave anything out?), and a young spinner who turned it square at medium pace to collect a 'lucky' seven wickets. As Les Ormes had lost to Jersey the day before, this meant that the series was all tied up at one game apiece, and Cricket Truly Was The Winner.

In the evening, we ate at another superb local restaurant, and watched the fireworks shepherd in the Bastille Day celebrations. Interestingly, the owners of the Chateau at Domaines des Ormes made it very plain that they wanted no truck with these peasant festivities. I'm not making that up. No wonder Zhou Enlai said it was still too early to assess the impact of the French Revolution.

What a brilliant trip. But I can look back on every

cricket tour I have made overseas (twelve, overall) with crystalline clear memories. There is no doubt that a common cause helps in the creation and sharing of these experiences, but cricket seems to provide a special cocktail of contest, tradition, strange clothes, eclecticism, and uninhibited enjoyment. The trip was slightly more sedate than some of the tours I took as a callow youth, when we would enforce a severe penalty system for undergraduate offences like using a designated (prohibited) word (eg. 'bat' or 'curry'), or not holding your drink in the official manner prescribed for the day (eg. right hand with extended pinky). But even as mature village cricketers, in France we felt like young kids on a school camp.

In order to produce a winning team from the weekend's battles, we did toy on the last evening with trying to develop some form of countback formula. Unfortunately, our only mathematician was Guy Peppiatt, the bookie, and he was busy wandering about trying to cadge money for a drink, after having been so comprehensively legged over by the skipper...

·11·

Pre-Season Training
Shiplake College Indoor Nets, Henley, Winter 2003

'It's probably true that hard work never killed anyone, but I figure why take the chance?'
Ronald Reagan

I wasn't sure that there would be a place for pre-season training in these essays. While Turville Park does engage in a formal pre-season cobweb-clearing program, it is rather more frenzied than the pace we are used to on Sunday aftenoons during the season proper. Pre-season practise is also a lot less unique. The romance of our pitch at Turville Heath does not readily translate to a sweaty school gym outside Henley in January. But the experience *is* instructive in the way that it helps to define the total village cricket adventure. It is also a useful opportunity to discuss the cricket vacuum that is the off-season. For a relationship which becomes so intense in the Summer, it is remarkable how abruptly and totally we are abandoned in the Winter. This does of course help to explain why pre-season training is so much more popular than it (or the skipper) has any right to expect. For those who are curious about why I am only dealing with this subject now, I should own up that it is a cheap theatrical trick. It is also, however, helpful to know a little about some of the key characters.

In early January, when Manchester United have normally throttled the life out of the Premiership Title race, we receive our first Turville news for over three months. The Secretary, David Cairns, and Captain, Paul Girdler write to tell us excitedly that a new season of cricket beckons. We can all begin pretending that Winter is over by attending the first Indoor training session on the last Tuesday in January. In his 2003 letter, Paul takes the gratuitous opportunity to hope that, by the time training starts, Australia has not won the Cricket World Cup then unfolding in South Africa. Not only does Australia crush Paul's optimism by cruising to victory, it goes the extra distance to beat England in Port Elizabeth, thereby tipping it out of the World Cup, and Nasser Hussain out of the English captaincy. This, in a match which means nothing to Australia in the context of the competition, but which nevertheless inspires them to one of the greatest batting comebacks ever seen. This happy confluence of events naturally guarantees my attendance at every single pre-season training session.

I am careful not to be too boastful. One of my earliest cricketing memories is of John Snow terrorising Australia to help England regain The Ashes in 1970-1971. I took this very, very personally. A little like the way Nick Hornby speaks of his totally obsessive support for Arsenal in the bible for sad supporters everywhere, 'Fever Pitch'. I am unable however to resist some judicious taunting of my team mates, and I prepare some pithy put downs. Cruelly, even this pleasure is diminished by the typical Englishman's predilection for slagging off his own team, before I can get my insults in.

In any event, I am officially launched on my sabbatical, and while I have started work on my thesis, I have the time, and the overwhelming urge to attend training. With our season not due to start until late April, we are facing 12 practice sessions. That's 24 hours of very intensive physical activity. I would be surprised if I expended this much time on concentrated physical effort during the whole cricket season. This is self evidently a ludicrous amount of time to devote to an activity that is more metaphysical than physical. Twenty four hours of lectures on Plato, Descartes and Schopenhauer would equip us better for the struggles ahead.

Believe me, pre-season training *is* both intense and concentrated. This makes it painful, and, except for the blissful time when you are batting ('10 minutes? ... that was never 10 ...!'), highly unrewarding. The culprit is of course bowling. The bowling action is not one you have had cause to execute since the previous September, except perhaps when falling off a tow lift while skiing in France (*poseur* alert). Most importantly, you are supremely unfit. Why on earth do you therefore believe that your body is capable of one hour and 50 minutes of bowling on a flat, hard surface? Because you forget how much it hurt last year. Because you are desperate to compensate for your slothful Winter. Because this is CRICKET, AT LAST! But most crucially, you have no choice, because there are only eight people at practice. This is too many for one net, but not enough for two. The skipper (a bowler) opens up two nets and, once you have had your bat, there is no escape. You are instantly transformed from Contemplative Family Man into Human Bowling Machine. Next morning, the pain is excruciating, but you try to persuade yourself that it is a badge of honour, the price you pay for this special calling. Sadly, you only ever see eight people at a pre-season training session. These stoics are drawn in turn from a constant pool of only about 10-12 people (from our official player list of 61 players). Bizarrely, two or three of our pre-season training complement you will then never see for the whole of the season. This defies explanation.

One of the other more interesting features of pre-season training is that not only is it long, but it is totally useless. Practising indoor, under lights, on hard bouncy surfaces, means we are preparing ourselves for conditions which bear only a passing resemblance to village cricket in April (and for much of the year, come to that). Bouncy wickets do however produce a curious reaction from many of our bowlers, who take an inordinate amount of pleasure from planting melon sized bruises on the inside thigh of a) the skipper, and b) anyone with pretensions to batsmanship. This seems to be sheer unadulterated male bitchiness, and must say something significant about the masculine condition. Unfortunately, as a man, and a cricketer, I am not permitted to discuss this any further with you.

Finally, pre-season practise is useless because we have all left our cricket text books at home. Invariably, we prefer to practise slog shots which we have seen on television during the most recent One Day Series. Who knows when we might be called on to smash six 6's in the last over, to win a stunning victory against our desperate rivals at Stonor?

During those rare moments when we are able to converse during practise, and of course more fulsomely in the bar afterwards, what do we say about our enforced separation during the Winter? And how do we rationalise the siren call of this game, and our passion for inflicting such pain on ourselves during these training sessions? Well of course, we don't. We talk about English football (mostly), English rugby (union), English cricket (sadly) and English girls (just kidding). Sometimes we stray into matters of work, but this is rare, and usually slightly uncomfortable. Life changing developments (changed jobs, married, elected Prime Minister) seem only to emerge in conversation by accident. This reticence to talk about more profound or personal issues is not simply a function of my 'new chum' status. In my three years I have helped to prop up many a bar as part of conversations involving groups of half a dozen or so. Once, a conversation strayed dangerously into politics (not particularly controversial - 'William Hague is a twat' sort of thing). My interlocutor seemed both liberated by this new topic of conversation, but at the same time fearful that his team mates might notice, and drive him from the pack.

On occasion, I have gently tried to engage my team mates on why they love cricket. I am surprised by the variety of reactions. They include - 'because I am exposed to such an interesting range of people I wouldn't otherwise get to meet' (except on tour with the Barmy Army presumably), 'because it is strange and beautiful' (as good as it gets, I think), 'it's like an organised weekly social event where I can get some exercise in good company' (simple, really), 'I actually hate it with a passion' (this from Barnaby, who had missed two stumpings the day I asked), 'why do you need to ask?' (because I'm writing a book and should have told you, sorry), 'because it's jolly' (not nearly as inadequate as it might seem at first blush), 'because it's there (Turville Park, that is), and because I still can' (a no-nonsense farmer, obviously).

There is also a reliable sense of bravado in our pre-season (and off-season) conversations. You may know the type of thing - 'We should organise a better/longer/different overseas tour this year', 'We should tell the skipper to give the ball to someone else occasionally', 'We should field a football team in the Winter to help us through the off-season'. None of this ever comes to pass of course, for the simple but obvious reason that there is no one at Turville called 'We should' to arrange these things.

Many of these recollections are mirrored in my Australian pre-season experiences. Australians do however tend to be more open about their personal situations. Not because they care more, but simply because they are more guileless about asking dumb but honest questions ('so tell me again how your girlfriend took up lap-dancing?'). On the other hand, pre-season training at the Singapore Cricket Club, whilst conducted Indoors (like Turville) took place entirely within the confines of the Club's Mens Bar (over-looking our two dilapidated and rather forlorn practise nets). As a result, I can't remember a thing we talked about, although I'm fairly confident it was arrant, gin and tonic fuelled nonsense.

After what seems an interminable lead up, pre-season finally becomes season proper. I am sorer (but fitter), wiser (about football, if not my team mates' domestic arrangements), and much, much happier. Now if I could only manufacture a decent slower ball at next years pre-season training. With any luck this will allow me to follow up with a quicker ball which surprises Jamie Hunt, and repays him for the internal bleeding he inflicted on my right leg this year …

·12·

Afternoon Tea

Turville v. Woodcote, Sunday, 22 June, 2003

'All the recipes have been tested by Mary ...'
**Introduction to 'Cream Cakes and Boundaries -
Village Cricket Tea Recipes'**

You may have thought that the quaint tradition that is English village cricket Afternoon Tea was either too precious, or too easy, to lampoon. Right on both counts. But you have to give me credit for resisting for so long.

The occasion for this particular collection of observations was provided by my debut appearance as Match Manager for the game against Woodcote at home. In only my third season with Turville, I was being entrusted with the pavilion keys, the kit, and team selection. A heavy burden. A quick check of the Club records (I asked Mike Wicks, Club conscience) suggested that this was some sort of record for a Melburnian.

Even more portentous of course was the responsibility I (that is to say Ruth) was being charged with to furnish a respectable Afternoon Tea. But while my team mates were thinking of shrimp cocktail with perhaps a nice light Hunter Valley sauvignon, I was in the Vegemite sarnie and lime cordial camp. Thankfully, Ruth had more imagination than me. She also had more charm and grace (without ever playing cricket?).

The tradition of Afternoon Tea in village cricket is obviously ancient, and one which I am loathe to challenge. But ... why? I mean, what for? What the bloody hell is it all about? Sensible adults have all had their lunch before the game, say at 1.00pm. Tea is a mere three and a half hours later. In the intervening period, most of us have gone through the following typically arduous program - driven to the ground, got changed, fielded (or faced) a handful of balls, and returned to the pavilion with an inexplicable but overwhelming appetite.

As a caution to any of us who were not disposed to take the custom seriously, the Turville Clubhouse displayed a recent news story (affixed to the wall above the kettles, naturally) describing the fate of Stoke Canon Cricket Club of Exeter. Here was a cricket club with a relatively modern history (founded 1978), which had been forced to fold after the wives and girlfriends withdrew their afternoon tea services. This resulted in the lads endeavouring to do the necessary. The outcome was curried egg, marmite and peanut butter sandwiches. Opposing teams were said to be appalled, and one by one fixtures simply disappeared.When the Club ultimately gave up, it is reported that they spent the surplus funds (£200) on 'a good night out'. That sounds to me like 20 jugs of beer to wash down all the leftover Marmite sandwiches.

Having not paid much attention to the details of this grand tradition at Turville in the past, I am instructed by

Ruth to make copious notes in the weeks leading up to the Woodcote game. Number of sandwiches, quality of fillings, shape and texture of cakes, outfits worn by wives and girl-friends ('again ... really?!'). Ruth's experience in Australia was to serve up a doorstopper size chocolate mud cake, which was more than enough for young lads labouring in 42 degree heat. In Singapore, she was accustomed to sitting on the balcony sipping Margaritas, while the Cricket Club staff attended to our every whim.

Singapore teas were a real treat. There was a nodding reference to tradition with cucumber sandwiches and scones. But the real attraction was in the local dishes - Mee Goreng, Beef Rendang, Mulligatawny Soup and Chicken Laksa. This would have been perfect but for the fact we had been in the field in sweltering 30 degree heat. It finally dawned on me how the grand tradition of 'batting first' had evolved. You know the rule - as a captain, if you win the toss, nine times out of ten you bat first. The other time you think about bowling first, but then you bat anyway. It was all to do with the Englishman's digestive processes.

Thankfully, I was able to render considerable assistance in the Tea Duties. I bought a book. To those of you who are keen to gain a closer understanding of the tradition, I recommend 'Cream Cakes and Boundaries - Village Cricket Tea Recipes'. It will set you back 99p (truly!) but in 116 pages, Charmaine Hutton has compiled the authoritative reference work in this field (alright, the only reference work). It ranges from the traditional (Scones, from Kent; Bakewell Tart, from Surrey; and Anzac Biscuits, from Devon), to the functional (Microwave Lemon Cake, from

Yorkshire), the exotic (Tabbouleh, also, intriguingly, from that hotbed of multiculturalism, Yorkshire), and finally, Outback Pie, contributed by one Mr Richie Benaud from Sydney. Marvellous, that.

It was in the beverage department that we suffered perhaps our biggest shock. We were surprised enough to find recipes for home made Pimm's, Sloe Gin and West Indies Rum Punch (with the clearly redundant warning to 'Enjoy With Caution'), but the section on 'Tea' was a revelation. So that there can be no misinterpretation, I recite relevant extracts from the instructions verbatim -

'Allow 1 standard sized tea bag per person in a large tea pot ... some people might prefer coffee ... So have a jar of coffee handy'

Tea bags! Coffee! How can this be proper? Does the MCC know, do you think? Although taken aback, I was at least encouraged to think that perhaps other traditions (Declaration Cricket, Leg Before Wicket, Teasing the Quaint Australian's Accent) might also one day be toppled.

Turville's match against Woodcote turns out to be a quite typical example of this fascinating English ritual, although it followed a most untypical Turville cricketing performance. As Match Manager, I had struggled to finally marshal 11 players, of which three were ring-ins, and four were genuine duffers. As usual, one player cried off on the Saturday, leaving us with a tenuous 10. One of my ring-ins was Jon Morcom, a chum who I had started playing cricket with at age 11 in Melbourne. Having last pulled on his creams (now 'yellows') seven years ago, Jon needed a substantial number of blandishments to trek up to Henley from London, where he was now living. In the 'trim, taut and terrific' stakes, his comfortably fitting gear meant that he at least had 'taut' well and truly mastered. His assessment the next day was broadly one of 'you bastard, get me an osteopath', tempered however by a view of our ground and setting as 'idyllic beyond a cricket fanatic's wildest dreams'. And maybe, just maybe, I might be able to call on him again if in need.

Jamie Hunt was captain for the day in Paul's absence, and after winning the toss it was agreed that it made sense to bat first given our modest resources. In a complete day out, Jamie and I put on a 250 partnership (my first 100 on the hallowed Turville wicket), to carry us to 265-2. Ruth thought I only stayed out in the middle to avoid preparing the tea. Luckily, our daughters Harriet (11) and Prudence (10) were along for the day to help out. My teenagers, Georgia and Thomas, were otherwise engaged in growing up activities. It is a tricky thing, developing into a spectacular human being, but all the while looking 'cool' as you do it. Remarkably, helping out with Afternoon Tea at the cricket was not very 'happening'. Harriet and Prudence's assistance came largely in the form of climbing Turville's sycamore tree, fighting over who was to read the latest Harry Potter first, and spilling the tea.

After Turville declared its innings closed, everyone repaired to the Club rooms to test the rustic Australian's first efforts at refuelling hungry village cricketers. Ruth had settled on Hummingbird Cake (Banana, Pineapple, Mango and Indian Spices - that'll show 'em - Nigella eat your heart out), together with scones and jam and cream - as a sop to the English, Vegemite sandwiches - as a sop to me, Chocolate Cake - as a sop to the old days in Melbourne, and some elaborately constructed savoury croissants (a sop to the French?). All complemented by tea from the Club's industrial sized tea pots, which were last washed in 1968, the Year of The Great Tea Trolley Disaster. After a few anxious moments with Club curmudgeon John Hancock in relation to a modest amount of tea which had regrettably been spilled on several saucers by Prudence (Presentation is apparently a key element of the tradition), the event was declared a success, with almost all of the dainties being hoovered up.

As always, at Afternoon Tea there is strictly no mixing between teams. Much like the distinct segregation of sexes that is commonplace at an Australian BBQ. It's obviously not enough that on a typical match day we spend up to eight hours together (including time at the pub). I guess it's probably reasonable that we remain apart from the opposition at tea given the psychological fervent(!) that inevitably precedes the rejoining of formal battle. One of the more amusing stories at this Tea emerged from a match at Turville just the day before, when a swarm of bees suddenly invaded the pitch from our magnificent sycamore tree, causing some consternation. As Englishmen, my team mates were sensible enough to remain still until the threat from these marauding insects (clad in their smart cricket colours) had passed. A similar episode in Australia would have seen 11 fielders, 2 umpires and 2 batsmen running around with arms flailing, screaming 'F… off you little C…s!'.

So, with battle rejoined after Ruth's Tea-time triumph, we manage to dismiss Woodcote for 165 to carry off a most satisfying victory. I complete my Match Manager duties by packing the kit (last undertaken in 1982 based on the Falkland's War headlines I could read in the 'Daily Telegraph' I fished out from the bottom of the heap), filling in the Match Report for the 'Henley Standard' (I hope they don't need any more than 10,000 words), and grovelling comprehensively to John Hancock for having prepared such a wonderful pitch for our match.

This just leaves me with the problem of how to get the children to help me eat the mountain of left over Vegemite sandwiches. Bloody heathen Englishmen …

·13·

English Weather

Turville v. Medmenham, Wednesday, 18 June, 2003

'Tomorrow, expect rain clearing to leave
heavy showers.' (?)
Daily Mail, 29 July 2003

Having unashamedly poked fun at English Afternoon
Tea, I now feel fortified in my desire to explore that other
staple of English cricket fickleness, The Weather. Once
again, it might be felt that this is just too easy, and moreover
that there couldn't possibly be any more to say on a feature
of life in the British Isles which has been maligned so
widely. In my defence, I would offer the following justifi-
cations for revisiting the topic. First, cricket is an outdoor
game, which in England brings weather into the overall
equation as in no other place in the world, particularly on
village cricket grounds of variable quality. Second, because
I hail (I'm reliably informed that one pun is all I will be
allowed) from Melbourne, which has spawned bestseller
songs like 'Four Seasons in One Day' for very sound and
obvious reasons. Third, because it's my Diary.

It is also fair to say that I have witnessed some remarkable weather related cricket phenomena in many different

parts of the world. A good proportion of these have occurred in the Tropics, where the combination of heat and over-zealous refreshment often lead to serious misjudgements. None more ridiculous perhaps than the Six-A-Side competition at the Gymkhana Club in Chiang-Mai, Thailand's second biggest city, in 1989. It doesn't bear thinking about how such a strongly contested event came to be situated in this most unlikely location for cricket, bang in the middle of Asia. Teams from Australia, New Zealand and India (amongst other countries) were participating, many with former Test Players. The sponsor of the Tournament was Steinlager, the New Zealand brewer. This was perhaps the biggest clue to what unfolded at the end of an innings shortly after mid-day on Day Two. An over enthusiastic spectator decided at this moment to launch himself over the modest three foot high fence, and charge off across the field in the blazing sun. With no clothes on. The crowd of perhaps 200 were only moderately curious about this intrusion on to the pitch, until our streaker, a middle aged Englishman, attempted to leap over the stumps at the bowlers end (insert own pun here). At this point, our hero pulled a hamstring and fell to the ground as if he had been shot. It was clear he wasn't going to get up. It was equally clear that we were not leaving the comfort of the beer tent to render assistance in the 40 degree heat. Eventually, our limp exhibitionist was rescued by his wife or girlfriend, who had been waiting dutifully on the other side of the ground with his clothes (that's right, stupid *and* pre-meditated). They hobbled off into the jungle together, never to be seen again.

I am very happy to proclaim up front that English weather gets unjustifiably bad press. As readers will have already discerned from my earlier accounts, much of my cricket has been played in spectacular conditions. In June 2003, the temperature in London reached at least 20 degrees Celsius *on every single day*. (August, in turn, even produced the hottest day on record. Over 37 degrees - the first time the mercury had breached 100 degrees Fahrenheit. One Bureau Meteorologist described it as an 'honour' to be working on such an historic occasion - clearly his office was air-conditioned.)

But none of this seems to prevent the English from stoically ignoring the facts, and trotting out one of two typical responses - 'Oh it will change soon enough', or 'About time, you should have seen it last year' (I did. It was equally clement). Not only is the heat bearable (typically 20-22 degrees) but the absence of hot gusting winds is a remarkably pleasant change from Australia. Perhaps most importantly, very few games have been interfered with by the weather conditions. Here's a slightly heretical thought. If you strip out the games abandoned to weather without a ball being bowled, then I believe that the English climate is much more pleasant (and conducive) for cricket. The (much) hotter weather in Australia, the West Indies, South Africa and the sub-Continent does, however, inevitably make for cricketers who are better prepared for the conditions which generally obtain in Test Cricket.

The biggest weather related bugbear in this country is not so much the cold in April and September, but simply that official weather forecasting is performed by Ouija Board.

The clarity of forecasts (forget about reliability) is perfectly enigmatic. In Australia of course, it is simply 'Melbourne - 32 degrees and overcast. Possible bushfires, so be bloody careful'. The English equivalent (and remember, this is a country which would fit comfortably into Queensland - several times over) often anticipates three different weather patterns (sunny, wet, windy) in one afternoon *and* it attempts to do this for everyone's street. It's true. On the BBC website, I can get a local weather forecast for my district by plugging in *my postcode*. But don't even think about looking beyond tomorrow. That's when it gets really complicated. This could well be the legacy of Michael Fish, the BBC weather presenter, who famously said, 24 hours before the onset of major hurricane activity in England in 1987, that we could expect some sunny, wet and windy weather (depending on your particular postcode). Woops.

Even more problematic in the English Summer is of course the mass emigration of players on their annual holidays. The holiday season seems to be a greater problem in this country, although I suspect it is probably a function of my more mature, and therefore more affluent Turville team mates driving (and flying) the consumer led economic miracle (usually all the way to Provence or Tuscany). We faced this problem in Singapore every cricket season in much the same way. English expatriates all fled the island nation in August to be back in Europe with their families (and often, with their children, who were boarding in England). Looking back now to my Report in the September 1989 edition of 'The SCC [Singapore Cricket Club] Magazine', the problem was obvious -

'As you might expect, a hectic month of cricket [August] has unhappily co-incided with Summer Holidays, bogus injuries, periods of domestic/family conscience, and demonstrations of unfortunate temperament'.

I suspect the 'unfortunate temperament' was in fact mine, as I struggled to put two sides on the field every Sunday. If I could have just married up the two way flows of holiday season immigration and emigration, then I might have solved the perennial Summer player availability tribulations once and for all.

The Medmenham game is in fact a good news story about English weather, and - as Turville's one and only Limited Overs game for the year - bears on other issues we have covered. After an unbroken spell of six days of fine weather, the game against Medmenham looked like co-inciding with the eventual change, and therefore being a much more limited overs game than we would have liked. This was a Wednesday evening game of twenty overs a side, and all day I watched the leaden sky threaten to break. I set off for Turville under the same heavy sky and, sure enough, by the time I arrived, I had both headlights and windscreen wipers in action. This proved to be only the fringe of the front, however, and so we were able to make a start shortly before 6.30pm. We won the toss and batted, still feeling reasonably confident that we might have some fun, and then get down to the pub when the rain did eventually arrive (before having to engage in any messy fielding and bowling).

Naturally, the weather did the very opposite of what we expected, and the skies brightened enough for us to get our match finished comfortably by 9.00pm. Turville compiled 132 from its 20 overs, due in large part to an effortless 81 from Jamie Hunt. This, after a long day in the field (the other field - on his father's farm), and shortly before we sent him back out with the new ball to bowl Medmenham out. Unfortunately, Medmenham were never really troubled in overhauling our total with four overs to spare, thanks to some big hitting from them and some rubbish fielding from us. In our defence, while the light had improved, it was still cool, so there were some judiciously withdrawn hands from what might, in 20 degree conditions, have been regulation catches.

On the other hand, there was no defence for my first spell of bowling for six weeks - 37 runs off three overs. The greatest indignity was to have been reverse swept for four in my last over. While I'm not fast, I'm fast enough that this piece of effrontery did dislodge a 'sledge' from my throat (of the 'how do you expect me to explain this to my children' variety). I consoled myself with the excuse that I was still a bit rusty on returning from a painful shoulder injury ('Well Mr Wade, I've got some good news and bad news. First, there are no exercises needed for this injury, second, all you need is to undo 43 years of crap posture … Next! …').

Remarkably, after finishing our game the skies cleared, and the night became almost balmy. We were able to spend the rest of the evening (until about 11pm) in the beer garden at the Fox & Hounds, most of us in shorts and T-shirts, discussing the beating we had just taken at Medmenham's hands. On reflection, maybe a Declaration game might have been more sensible ...

·14·

English Villages
Turville v. Hambleden, Sunday, 6 July, 2003

''Turville': from the old English 'thyrre' and 'feld'
meaning 'dry open land''.
South Oxfordshire District Council Website

British village name spotting (and parodying) is a tried and trusted pastime. And for good reason. It's first-rate fun. So, to get this out of the way quickly, my personal favourites include Giggleswick, Pratt's Bottom, Little Snoring, Biggleswade (no relation), Bottom-in-the-Beans, and its near neighbour (physiologically at least), Shellow Bowells.

It would be remiss of me not to talk a little about some of the quaint villages which appear on Turville's fixture card. The game I have chosen to lead this discussion is Hambleden, an old rival and near neighbour. This is not, it should be noted, the Hambledon in Hampshire, regarded by many as the cradle of modern cricket. This is the Oxfordshire Hambleden which, on the scale of accepted village cuteness, is right up there, providing the setting for the movie 'Chitty Chitty Bang Bang' for example. In fact, the village had acquired a reputation as the 'Hollywood of the Home Counties'. Scenes from 'Sleepy Hollow', 'The Avengers' and '101 Dalmations' have also taken advantage of this magical and quite secluded village, set back from the main Marlow-Henley Road. A charming square provides the focal point for the village, bounded by an imposing Norman church (St. Mary of the Virgin) which towers over the hamlet. The High Street and various brick-and-flint cottages, houses and shops are all beautifully preserved and presented. They include the impressive birthplace of Lord Cardigan, he of Light Brigade, and futile but romantic charges at fixed Russian gun emplacements, fame.

Season 2003 was in fact a traumatic one for our friends at Hambleden, as their village had been put up for sale by the landlord, the W.H. Smith family, famous for its chain of high street newsagents cum bookstores. The agents were looking for a sum reportedly in excess of £30m for the 1,666 acres of countryside, farms, shoot (patronised by Prince Andrew and Jackie Stewart, amongst others), houses, cottages, pub (the wonderful 'Stag & Huntsman') and village store. The sale was in the no doubt capable hands of agents FPD Savills, and their representative Mr. William Duckworth-Chad, which is a real name to conjure with. Should the Duckworth-Lewis One Day cricket scoring formula have been invoked to settle Al Gore's hanging chad problems in Florida? I can't be the only person asking these crucial questions, surely?

I remember visiting the Stag & Huntsman one afternoon to canvas local opinion first hand. It was at this point that I was introduced to the bizarre custom in this pioneering country of closing pubs like this between 2.30pm and

6.00pm in the afternoon. Nevertheless, I did manage to learn that the press were already speculating on potential buyers for the Estate. David Beckham was an early favourite (to add to his Buckinghamshire property, known as 'Beckingham Palace'), until he turned his attention to villas in Spain, rather than villages in the Thames Valley.

In the light of all of this uncertainty, it is understandable that the Hambleden players were perhaps not entirely focussed on the second of our two fixtures against them in 2003 at their (or rather, W.H. Smith's) home ground in July.

The sheer history that oozes from some of these villages can be distracting for someone like me who is already one-fifth as old as his native country (or at least Anglo-Saxon settlement in his native country). Britwell Salome, another nearby Oxfordshire village, and Turville rival, traces its name back to 1086 (shortly after the Normans had launched their extended touring party in England). The name comes from the old English 'Brutwelle' meaning spring or stream of the Britons. Salome was added in honour of the de Suleham family in the 13th century. History does not record what de Suleham thought about Declaration Cricket.

Our fiercest adversaries at Stonor Cricket Club represent a village (with roots deriving from the Stonor family estate) enjoying a long and fascinating history. This includes the prominent role played by Stonor Park manor as a refuge and underground printing press for persecuted Catholics like Edmund Campion (later Saint Edmund Campion). This followed the painful split in the Church after Henry VIII was excommunicated by the Pope in 1533. This split must have been almost as agonizing as the wedge driven into the Hunt family when young James Hunt elected to move up the road from Stonor to Turville to play his cricket 460 years later.

I suspect a large part of the Stonor cricket team's belligerence might come from its patrons' difficult history. The Stonors were 'recusants', refusing to take the Oath of Supremacy which made the reigning monarch the head of the English Church. Dame Martha Stonor was imprisoned for this principle in 1581, and a substantial part of the vast Stonor lands were either confiscated, or sold off, to fund the enormous fines levied by the Crown on the family during this period. Happily, this did not include the cricket ground, which still stands proudly and serenely opposite the main gates. Today, Thomas Stonor, the seventh Lord Camoys, is patron of Stonor Cricket Club, while his son and heir, William, is the Club President.

Oxfordshire has always been known not only as a redoubt for Catholics, particularly at the time of the Reformation, but also as a Loyalist Shire, with Oxford acting as the temporary Royal capital during the Civil War in 1642. A rather listless period at deep cover during the Hambleden game had me comparing Oliver Cromwell with modern era cricketers. The best I could do was an amalgam of Ian Botham and Ian Chappell (for irreverence to established institutions), with perhaps a bit of W.G. Grace and Don Bradman (megalomania), and Denis Compton and Richie Benaud (for the necessary mugging for the cameras) thrown in. Geoff Boycott actually graced the Turville pitch in 1981 during the period of his suspension from first class cricket, so perhaps we should just settle for him as the archetypal Roundhead.

A number of our opponents are the result of the combination of two villages. One such is Brightwell cum Sotwell, which came together in 1948. It is described by the South Oxfordshire District Council as 'a good starting point for longer walks' to other places. This seems a less than glowing endorsement. Much like Singapore - once voted the 'Most Boring City in the World' by The Economist. One outraged correspondent (Singaporean, naturally) wrote that this simply could not be possible, as Singapore enjoyed a marvellous airport with excellent access to some really interesting places.

I am happy to say that the village of Brightwell cum Sotwell is in fact a picture postcard delight in its own right, with a smashing pub - The Red Lion - holding a commanding position on the village's very private high street.

As we have seen, our own village of Turville derives its name from the old English words of 'thyrre' and 'feld' which together mean 'dry open land'. I think this is in turn a reference to that spot down at deep third man, where tailend batsmen keep snicking the ball over the head of the slips fielders off my bowling. The village also has something of a 'star' quality, providing the Church (another 'St.Marys') and setting for the BBC television series 'The Vicar of Dibley'. There are many rich parallels here, such as the elegant but cautious David Weston, assuming the alter ego of 'Jim' when calling for a quick single - "no, no, no, no ... yes". The earnest character of 'Frank Pickle' could easily be a suitable motif for a routine Turville batting collapse (as in, "that were a Frank Pickle ..."). Or perhaps we could nick one of Dawn French's cast off cassocks to use as a sight-screen at the Turville end? Whatever the case, prayer is something which we may need to call on for our next Stonor Derby.

I learned a little more of Turville's history at an exhibition at the Wycombe Museum in August 2003 with the catchy title of 'Cricket Past and Present Across the Wycombe District'. While not necessarily expecting to encounter a sell out crowd at this blockbuster showing, I was surprised to see only one car (the curator's) in the Museum car park when I visited. It was a surprisingly rich exhibition. Apart from immaculately maintained score-books from the 1890's, and a photo of an early Turville team taken in 1910, it was interesting to discover that Turville Park Cricket Club began life not as a village team, but as an Estate team, raised from workers on the Turville Park Estate owned by the O'Brien-Hoare family. This is the Estate which is now owned by Lord Sainsbury. Over time, Turville Park became the natural village team. Sadly, it is no longer customary to be smoking a pipe for team photos.

The 'big smoke' around these parts (not counting Oxford, which is further up the M40 than we reach on our fixture card) is Henley. We play an annual game against the Henley Cricket Club, but this does not always prove to be especially satisfactory. HCC plays the bulk of its games in the local league, and is therefore much more result-driven. Amazingly, afternoon tea is not the centrepiece of the Henley team's day.

The town of Henley itself is one of my favourites. It is old, predating what the Henley Town Council quite unself-consciously describes as 'The Conquest' (I assume this refers to 1066, rather than HCC's first win against Turville). And it is beautiful, with narrow winding streets and splendidly preserved Tudor shops and residences. Alas, the narrow winding streets are not coping very well with the ever increasing volumes of traffic.

Henley also takes full advantage of the River Thames, which explains why the Henley Royal Regatta has been such a popular local attraction since 1839. It is notable that Thomas Stonor was a co-founder of the Regatta. This was shortly after the Catholic Emancipation Act of 1829 was passed, allowing Catholics to once again hold public office. The rowing Regatta transforms Henley for five days every year, as over 500 crews (including more than 100 from overseas) compete in 19 separate events over the fixed course of one mile and 550 yards. The format is unique, being a knock out draw with only two boats in every heat. This can mean up to 100 races a day on some days. Perhaps this is where the Henley Cricket Club draws its competitive instincts from. It is also notable that prize givers at the Regatta over the years have included royalty (for example, Sir Pelham Warner and Lord (Colin) Cowdrey), as well as a number of those ubiquitous Windsors.

Finally, Henley is an important place for a Melbourne friend and former team mate, the stalwart St. Andrews Cricket Club wicketkeeper, Bill Birch. On a visit to London in 2001, Bill was anxious to come up to see us because we were close to Henley, and a famous shrine of which, heretofore, we had been blissfully unaware. So we made the pilgrimage to Dusty Springfield's grave at Henley's 18th century St. Mary of the Virgin Church, and Bill's humming behind the stumps for all those years in Melbourne finally came jarringly into focus.

But our opponents on this hot July day at Hambleden were obviously preoccupied by the impending sale of the village, and therefore not up for a serious battle. After losing the toss, we were put into bat. On this day, 27 degrees felt like 35, so it was a good toss to lose. Hambleden fits snugly into a valley in the Chilterns, and was not favoured by any freshening breezes. I was captaining on this occasion after our official office bearers had exhausted all the usual excuses (roughly, 'I couldn't be shagged'). Jamie Hunt's excuse was particularly troubling. Wedding anniversary. It was his first anniversary, so allowances were made, but recidivism obviously cannot be tolerated. Barnaby made a flying visit during the afternoon, but this turned out to be for the purpose of tampering with the score book to (properly) attribute a catch to himself from the previous day's play (and treat us to an extended description of its virtuosity).

By the end of 38 overs Turville had posted 245-7, on a pitch which sloped alarmingly, but behaved responsibly. In reply, Hambleden looked like a team more focussed on how to marshal £30m (perhaps I should have been more worried about having left my wallet in my kit?). They never attempted to tackle our target, even though Turville bowled every one of its players (except the keeper, Colin Simon, and even he was invited to have a turn). Our opponents meandered to 130 for the loss of only five wickets. It was perhaps fitting, in a strangely perverse way, that my first outing as captain resulted in such a disappointing draw. Oh, and I was given out LBW.

Despite the frustrating outcome, the cricket almost seemed like a sideshow. When I tossed the coin (in the shadow of the Manor House of the W.H. Smith family - which wasn't up for grabs, as it happens), my brief conversation with the opposing captain turned unerringly to the sale. All the talk at Tea was about the sale process which was down to one solid bid, with a competing consortium bid rumoured to be brewing (and running up against time constraints). The chat after the game was more of the same. Drinks were held that evening in the High Street at the 'Hambleden Institute & Sports Club'. The Clubhouse was determinedly labelled as 'Members Only'. It struck me as a rather forlorn hope on the part of the locals to keep the wider world out for as long as possible.

As it turns out (did Hollywood have a hand?), the village was withdrawn from the market in late July 2003. While the villagers were thrilled (the Smith family is regarded as a munificent landlord), Mr. Duckworth-Chad was reported to be 'disappointed' (now there's a surprise), and one of the bidding consortiums described the process as a 'bugger's muddle' (sounds a bit like the Hambleden batting line up).

Who knows, perhaps the spirit of Lord Cardigan lives on in the village, and the resistance offered by the locals to the sale was more successful than the Charge at Balaclava …?

·15·

Village Cricket Partners
Turville v. Ibstone, Sunday, 24 August, 2003

'Still, the suspicion persists that males secrete some
type of archetypal fluid that makes it easier for them
to understand what's at work here.'
Tom Callahan
(on boxing, actually)

'Yes you have', said Paul.

'No I haven't', I gently responded.

'You must have met her, What about ... er ...?' (rather meek collapse of position here).

'I'm sorry Paul, but I haven't yet had the privilege of meeting your fiancee'.

Almost at the end of my third year at Turville, and I had yet to meet the skipper's intended. While this left Paul slightly perplexed, it had not yet lessened my enjoyment of cricket at Turville. Nevertheless, on this thin pretext I decided to address the crucial question of how the gentle sex feels about a game which does not go out of its way to embrace it. I concede that this is a hugely ambitious project, perhaps even more mysterious than analysing the LBW law. I have already deployed a substantial number of words to provide only a semi-coherent picture of how (one) man feels about the game. But women? It is difficult to ignore the issue. Men sacrifice many hours for cricket, and in the process deprive their partners of time for doing, well, partnering things. It is rare that this deprivation causes any rancour or recrimination, and again I am keen to know, why?

I propose to tempt fate once more, by reducing this discussion to outrageous generalisations. First, some caveats. I am not speaking about women who play the game. Frankly, I don't know any. But even if I did, the fact that they play cricket would give them an insight which makes them quite different to the long-suffering (non-playing) partner. The following account will also inevitably appear to be condescending to some. The best I can say in my defence is that *I* don't fully understand cricket (although to be fair, I'm not even sure what I want to be when I grow up). I am therefore blowed if I can figure out what causes rational non-agitants to support this weird activity. So here is my attempt to interprete the unfathomable. My experience suggests that there are four main categories of cricket partner -

- ⊖ Genetic Supporter (28 per cent)
- ⊖ Duty Bound (29 per cent)
- ⊖ It's Cute/I Don't Understand It/I Can Change Him (12 per cent)
- ⊖ What Silly Boys (31 per cent)

Genetic Supporter

These partners have little choice. Typically born into a family of cricketers (father/brothers), they are exposed to the charms of the game from an early age. They also grow up in an environment where the inordinate amount of time devoted to the game is accepted as a matter of course. Ruth belongs to this class. Her father, Bob, played competitive cricket in a local Melbourne league for many years. And I mean *competitive* cricket. Bob's team was once threatened with ejection from the League for, shall we say, unstatesmanlike behaviour. Much later, during the interview process with Bob for his daughter's hand, I was the reluctant beneficiary of an extended explanation for this 30 year old outrage. I am pretty sure that I still would have secured Bob's consent even if I hadn't agreed to take up placards to march on the Melbourne South Suburban Cricket Association. The fact that I had played cricket from a very young age was also an important factor in winning Bob's affections. Poor Ruth, she never really had a chance.

As a result of my, and her father's, gentle education, Ruth does 'get' cricket as well as any woman I know. I am slightly chastened to have to admit that she appreciates village cricket even better. The fact that it appeals to her feminine instincts says something about the rather gentle pace of the game as it is played at Turville. But at the end of the day, I fear that it is still an inherited or genetic form of support, rather than an altogether cerebral one. When I pressed her once for her thoughts on the game, the reaction was instructive -

'it's long ... (extended, too thoughtful pause) ... *gracious, gentlemanly* (has she been reading my drafts?) ... *unsexy outfits'* (why the International Cricket Board continues to ignore this is a mystery to many of us)

Perhaps not terribly surprisingly, Ruth's nearest English counterpart is Felicity, wife of Barnaby. Felicity was also born into a cricketing family, although hers is a slightly different genetic strain. While her every action speaks of 'Land of Hope and Glory', I suspect that deep down she is sensible enough to know the terrible truth - that Barnaby and I are not really very good cricketers. As a result of her cricket pedigree, I trust her not to reveal this to anyone.

Duty Bound

This class of female supporter is, as the name would suggest, perhaps slightly more grudging. While the married state is not strictly required, the feeling is very definitely one of long term vows ('To Love, Honour and Accept, If Not Understand, The Need to Dedicate the Lord's Day of Rest to Declaration Cricket, Rather than To a Nice Drive in the Countryside'). This class often comprises partners from the next group ('I Can Change Him') who have failed.

Apart from losing their partner for whole days at a time, the 'duties' of this group are not terribly onerous. These partners can almost always be relied upon to offer up one or two smashing Afternoon Teas per season. Men are usually gracious enough to recognise this for the anachronism which it is (although this doesn't mean that they will necessarily help with the dishes). Intermittent support from the boundary line on a fine mid-summer's day, is another of the more prosaic yet pleasant responsibilities. No cricket knowledge is needed, or expected, to enjoy the sunshine.

Some partners, like Sara, Colin Simon's wife, take on more formal roles like Scoring. Even battle hardened village cricketers run a mile from scoring duties, so Sara is a real godsend. It involves long hours of concentration hunched over a desk, with a complicated and idiosyncratic book, tallying up random outcomes (like 'runs', 'wickets', and 'four wide no ball byes' - (?)) while interpreting arcane and silly signals from the umpire (like 'help, it's hot, get someone else to come out here will you?'). When I asked Sara once what she liked about cricket, she said it was 'nice to get out in the fresh air'. Here is someone who would seem to have an over-developed Churchillian take on duty. I gently backed away at this point, in case I inadvertently consumed some of 'her' fresh air.

I encountered a similar specimen at my Melbourne club, St.Andrews. At one Annual General Meeting we were working through the uncomfortable process of electing office bearers. You know the drill - 'any nominations for Secretary/Treasurer etc ...?' (much nervous shifting of feet and averting of eyes until the incumbent bravely agrees to carry on for another year. 'Just one more, mind', he says. Every year). The toughest spot to fill was always 'Social Secretary' (not, it should be noted, a role which exists at Turville - I suspect my English team mates would deride the Australian practice of 'formalising' fun). At all events, this is a role which males are spectacularly ill equipped for. It involves planning, organisation, financial acumen, social skills, and just a little flair. During the longer than usual pregnant pause at this year's AGM, while waiting for someone to step up for the Social Secretary role, one of the wives (what was she even *doing* there?) said 'I'll do it.' Instead of doing the sensible thing and rushing over to carry Marita on our shoulders triumphantly around the Church Hall, there was, disgracefully, another round of nervous feet shuffling. This was a fully fledged Committee role, you see. A female had never before held a Committee role in St. Andrews' 75 year history. She would be entitled to attend our Committee meetings, and discover, a) what a rubbish job we were doing of running the Club, and, b) what a lark we were having doing it.

Oblivious to all this (and to the niceties of the secret ballot process), our 'new' Social Secretary thanked everyone for the honour, marched up to the Committee table, and quelled the pathetic resistance which had ever so briefly threatened to erupt. It is hard to imagine a similar scenario where the gender roles might operate in reverse.

Finally, in this category of partner support, there is Turville's *wunderkind* James Hunt, who married his Felicity in Season 2002. Jamie concedes that Felicity did not grow up in a cricketing family, but there could be no mistaking the fact that she has married into one. Jamie modestly (but self-assuredly) observes that Felicity 'understands' the importance of cricket. This sounds to me like Felicity 'understands' cricket like she 'understands' breathing. It's something she has to do.

It's Cute/I Don't Understand It/I Can Change Him

For many girls who haven't enjoyed the sort of indoctrination offered by Ruth and Felicity's families, their first exposure to cricket often comes through a new boyfriend. At best, there is possibly a vague consciousness that cricket is both odd and boring. In the first full flush of courtship, this oddness is mistaken for 'cuteness'. This is combined (dangerously) with an absence of any real experience of why cricket has dominated their partner's leisure time from an early age. The result is a woman who - when they finally learn that their first instinct ('odd and boring') was right - either moves on (typically to someone a bit racier, like an actuary), or quietly vows to change their partner's leisure time preferences. These efforts at effecting change are almost always utterly, hopelessly, doomed.

This is one of the rare 'personal' issues which men actually talk openly about at the cricket. For example, it is commonplace to taunt team mates who are struggling on their mobile phones to explain to their partners why they can't join that dinner party in London until after 10pm. ('But we were invited over three months ago' she says. 'Aha, but I showed you the Fixture List nearly six months ago' our team mate replies, resolutely, but entirely irrelevantly). There almost seems to be a half-secret hope that perhaps one of these bright young girls will succeed. This would provide visceral evidence for the rest of us, of how manful we have been to have arranged our relationships in such a way as to place cricket first.

Our skipper, Paul Girdler, was in a relationship with his

fiancee where leisure time activities were yet to be sorted. He was playing a skilful game, but it is very tough to keep explaining away the loss of 50 per cent of the weekend (to cricket) as a passing fancy. As a paramedic, Paul's fiancée no doubt assumed that - as a last resort - there might be a surgical procedure.

In Australia, I remember one team mate who was struggling to balance cricket and a new girlfriend. He was also a committed fan of heavy metal music. When we asked him once about whether this music was, well, perhaps a little too one dimensional, he took offence. He even suggested that his favourite band (AC/DC) performed a number of ballads. 'Like what?' we asked him. 'She's Got Balls' was his preferred choice. What a romantic. We were always confident of his loyalty to the cricket club after that.

The arrival of children into a 'I Can Change Him' partnership typically causes renewed pressures on a player's commitment to his cricket club. If it's a boy, the player is usually able to get away with some palaver about playing on to preserve and guarantee the newborn heir's birthright. If it's a girl, continuing to turn out for cricket at the weekend will often require large sums of cash to change hands. A vacation on the Mediterranean (in the winter, naturally) should ordinarily do the trick. It is of course one of life's strange ironies that between us, Barnaby and I have produced five daughters (looks like Sardinia this winter), and one son (who considers cricket to be a cross between some weird Aztec sacrificial ritual, and train spotting).

Silly Boys

Surprisingly, not a bigger group. Cricket would struggle to stand up to analysis from a disinterested and intelligent reviewer (i.e. any woman). Thankfully, most women *are* interested, and can somehow be persuaded to suspend their normal powers of dispassionate scrutiny. Those who cannot be so persuaded, inevitably conclude that we are just 'Silly Boys.' Consider the evidence, they would say -

⊖ Women are excluded from participating (while I'm not sure that there is actually a formal law prohibiting woman from playing in the men's game, this would be no more likely to occur in village cricket, than for Glen McGrath to compose a sonnet to celebrate Michael Vaughan's ascension to the captaincy of the England Team).

⊖ It *is* long (Ruth got that bit right). There really is no way to sugar coat this. It is also notoriously difficult for males to defend or explain (as my own efforts have demonstrated). I believe that this elusiveness is actually part of the charm of cricket, but it is understandable why women are suspicious of something which can't be defined more precisely. Football's 'off-side' rule is a walk in the park compared to the LBW Law.

⊖ It is essentially an unsocial activity. Not only can't women play, but there are very few opportunities for women to engage in social intercourse with their partners and team mates, either during a match or otherwise. There is an exception to prove every rule, and in this case it is provided by Barnaby (of course). In a 1982 game between

Barney's then team, the Privateers, and the famous Hampshire Hogs, Barnaby decided to lob his marriage proposal at Felicity. This was clearly more social intercourse than most women would expect at the cricket. It was a perfectly sensible thing to do, Barney told me - Privateers had essentially won the game at that stage.

⊖ The gear is unflattering. When men have any opportunity to exercise innovation or imagination in their wardrobe, we generally end up with something like the orange and yellow MCC tie. Look at us. We can't even co-ordinate creams and whites.

⊖ The athletes who play the game are, well, somewhat unathletic looking. And don't just dwell on the poor specimens which inhabit village cricket. You only need to compare say David Beckham with Graham Gooch, or Ian Thorpe with Allan Border, to appreciate the force of this argument.

⊖ There is a distinct lack of action and results, in many different respects ('just explain the point of a drawn game again, darling ...?', or, alternatively, 'just explain again why the part for the broken motor mower still hasn't arrived from Latvia?').

Of this group, there are those who simply stay away, and then are those who come just often enough to showcase their resentment and hostility. Men have no concept of how to relate to this latter sub-set. All of the 'Silly Boys' camp subscribe to the Rita Rudner theory of time utilisation. Rita, a New York comedienne, was asked (in relation to having a family) how she felt about a friend who had been in labour for 24 hours. '24 hours!', Rita exclaimed. 'I don't even want to do something that feels *good* for 24 hours!' At the very least, the 'Silly Boys' camp can be consoled that their partners do not have any time to run a mistress on the side.

Nonetheless, this group forms the biggest threat to cricket, because they know the score. And they know we know they know.

•

I finally meet Amanda, Paul's fiancee, at Turville's fixture against Ibstone. Turville Park has never enjoyed a large supporter base, but we are severely embarrassed by the legion of Ibstone hangers-on who appear at our home ground for this game. Every Turville supporter who appears is fallen upon by the Turville cricketers, eager to demonstrate that we too can play a brand of cricket which draws people from miles around. Today, however, Ibstone are too strong, and win by five wickets on a pitch which produces another 350 runs.

Amanda arrives at Tea, and lifts our supporter numbers to six. I realise I *had* already met her before (ouch!). She is young, charming and largely unschooled in the traditions of cricket. After recovering from my embarrassment, I do my best, and explain how lucky she is to have found someone like Paul who is so talented, and such an indispensable part of the Turville community. This seemed to go well. Shortly after, however, I hear someone explaining the LBW Law to Amanda, and I knew all was lost. Maybe the Captaincy position could be opening up sooner than we expected ...?

·16·

The Business of Village Cricket

Turville v. Checkendon, Saturday, 26 April, 2003

'An economist is someone who sees something
working in practice, and asks
whether it could work in principle'
Stephen M. Goldfeld

If it is not plain already, let me be clear - there is not a single thing I would change about Village Cricket in general, and Turville in particular. Except for the format. And of course the LBW rule. Oh, alright, and maybe the captain. But otherwise, nothing. With this disclaimer, I thought it might nevertheless be fun to apply the disciplines of the Corporate world to a typical Turville game. I have used the opening game of our 2003 campaign as the basis for this analysis, because April matches usually provide such a heady mix of farce and time wasting. Like the vast majority of corporate meetings I have endured over the years.

For convenience I have performed my review under the timeless Marxist categories of 'Capital' (Finance and Property) and 'Labour'. In a similar time-honoured corporate practice, I have rendered a bill to Colin Simon, the Club Treasurer, for my report. It could have been much worse Colin - I couldn't interest McKinsey in co-writing this study with me.

Capital

Finance

The funding of a typical amateur cricket club is invariably a precarious thing. My Melbourne club St. Andrews was perennially on the verge of financial ruin, and I'm still not certain how the looming disaster reported on at every committee meeting never actually came to pass. On the other hand, the Singapore Cricket Club was floating on a sea of Corporate Membership money, and so we were never really troubled by grubby money matters. Mind you, the beer was bloody expensive.

Turville sustains itself through a combination of Annual Subscription (£25) and Match Fees (£5). This might seem a sensible formula given the rather irregular playing patterns of many on our list, but it was an ongoing nightmare for the Match Manager charged with collecting the £5. Checkendon was a typical example. Robert Gunn was the Match Manager, and after the game he gently reminded us to cough up the five quid. Responses were as follows -

'Have you got change for £20? £10? 3,000 Polish Zlotys? (Barnaby has obviously just returned from another business trip).'

'My money is in the car.'

'Are you going to the pub? - I'll give it to you there' (the consummation of this promise has never once been known to actually take place at Turville).

'I don't have any money.'

'Barnaby will give you £17.50 for him, me and John,

and then you will owe James £3.70'(?)

'Why don't we set it off against the jug you owe me for dropping that sitter of a catch off my bowling?'

'Sod off.'

Finally, I am able to shake Robert off with this last one. When he adds up his takings, he will inevitably be £20-£30 short, so he just kicks in the necessary.

Funding would be easier if we simply floated Turville Park Cricket Club plc. Why not? There were many more implausible enterprises floated during the dot com boom. We could certainly gussy up an attractive Prospectus with restful shots of the Turville Heath ground. Probably best not to include pictures of neighbouring livestock (images of 'sheep' and 'fleece' may be counter productive). Investors looking for some kind of return on their investment will, however, need to be somewhat more spiritually minded. Dividends would obviously include the right to share in the peace of mind that a day at Turville can bring (especially welcome for holders of worthless dot com shares). Securities Regulators might also appreciate our rural setting, although visions of closed gates and bolted horses could be discomfiting. Special bonuses might include a free LBW waiver, or an extra over bowling with the wind at one's back (usually the skipper's preserve).

Debt is not a realistic option. I know many bankers, and none of them would seriously entertain an overdraft for something which can not be explained in 25 words or less. I have already comfortably exceeded this limit. Village cricket is very much an activity which attracts the well worn observation - 'a bank is a place where they lend you an umbrella in fair weather, and ask for it back when it rains again'.

Property

Turville's major (tangible) balance sheet item is represented by its mouldy old kit. The type of thing that inhabits most amateur clubhouses, including the statutory pads with rusted buckles that no one has used since the era of eight ball overs, and six unmatched right hand gloves for left handed batsmen. This equipment has of course been fully written off, but - like Shell's infamous oil rig, the Brent Spar - no one is quite sure how to get rid of it. Perhaps we should be looking at options for sale and leaseback?

No, burning it all at our next Guy Fawkes night bonfire is a much more realistic option. This is how we disposed of the framework for the Clubrooms old loo's in 2001.

Unlike the traditional corporate office, where employees make an art form of nicking the company stationery, most Turville players bring their own kit to each game, studiously avoiding the Club equipment. I suppose private property is, after all, central to a capitalist system. There *is* a slightly 'socialist' streak manifested by the practice of sharing the same ball between the two sides. This naturally means that the side bowling first has the advantage of a new ball. It is not clear how this custom emerged, but it does help to explain why Paul Girdler, captain *and* opening bowler, prefers to bowl first.

Labour

Personnel

The key input to the success of cricket as a beacon of free enterprise is of course the 'labour' of the players. This labour is organised in teams which are matched against each other on a week by week basis. This is much the same formula as for companies which compete against each other in the marketplace, with one major difference. A cricket match involves very immediate and transparent competition, and the opposition is easy to identify. In the corporate world, the adversarial contest is not quite so direct, and the opposition not nearly as obvious. This will often cause competitive spirits to be turned inwards against one's own colleagues, particularly in large organisations. There is, I think, a very interesting case for sporting (or other) contests between the staff of major corporate rivals. This would almost inevitably make the competition more visceral. It would also beat the hell out of another round of those interminable internal Steering Committee meetings.

Turville is, of course, a mutual, or co-operative, organisation - responsible to its members through the Annual General Meeting. The Turville Committee acts on behalf of these members as the effective Board of Directors, and follows the accepted City practice of holding infrequent meetings, and then doing whatever it wants. This is ever more acceptable to Club members because, much like City Directorships these days, nobody really wants the responsibility of holding any office at Turville. Complaining from the sidelines is a grand tradition of cricket clubs everywhere.

The Chief Executive at Turville is, of course, our captain Paul Girdler. Paul is not really of the 'Neutron Jack' Welch school. He needs to do much more huffing and puffing if he wants a major Management book deal when he retires. And if you ever want a lesson in why matrix management is a doomed strategy, you just need to see the skipper shifting me three feet to the left at extra cover, while the bowler is at the same moment sending me to second slip.

I like to think that the batsmen represent Turville's senior management cadre. They are usually smart, elegant, and very capable of blaming other people (see, Fast Bowlers) when things aren't going Turville's way. Again, like Senior Management, batsmen wave a big stick, and are heavily protected against incoming threats. Batsmen also tend to go on to become captains.

Bowlers tend to be differentiated between Medium, Fast and Slow. Medium pace bowlers look a lot like Middle Management, in that they will never win a game on their own, but seem as a group to perform a generally useful job. You know you only need half as many, but can never be certain which half to jettison. Fast bowlers, on the other hand, are very clearly the factory floor, and they best embody Marxist philosophy that capitalism (cricket) is based on the exploitation of raw labour (fast bowlers), leading to class conflict (fast bowlers tend to sit broodily together at one end of the table at Afternoon Tea). Or this could just be a lot of nonsense. Finally, Spin bowlers remind me of the consulting fraternity in that they are usually costly, but occasionally help to produce something (like a spectacular catch on the boundary line) for which they are only incidentally responsible, but nevertheless expert at taking credit.

Wicket keepers merit a category all of their own, and for me the parallel is obvious. These chaps are the IT (Information Technology) experts who constitute a separate priesthood. This is because no one else really understands or cares how they operate, but we do know when the process breaks down (when the mainframe crashes, or when a stumping is missed). This invariably undermines the confidence of the whole organisation. And beware, the combination of Spin Bowlers (Consultants) and Wicket-keepers (Information Technology) can be a very, very costly affair. It is a complete co-incidence that Barnaby is both a keeper, and an IT systems analyst. I think.

And last, fielders are a bit like those important people in Customer Service, or Call Centres - crucial for the overall well being of the enterprise, but desperately uninteresting, so we should just let someone else worry about it. Fielding practise also has a clear corporate parallel, resembling those useless company 'training' sessions which have become so fashionable. Both activities tend to be performed under sufferance, with all participants thinking that everyone but themselves should be enduring this kind of suffering.

Rewards

The benefits of playing cricket at Turville are hopefully readily apparent by now. There are perhaps one or two things that need to be added to make the Club an 'Employer of Choice'. First, on cold days in April like the one at Checkendon, Health & Safety Regulations would surely prescribe that Slip fielders should be no more than decorative. The ball is hard, after all. In fact, slip fielders at the village cricket level remind me a lot of Non-Executive Directors, in being likened to bidets - it's not entirely clear what they are for, but they do lend a certain touch of sophistication. Second, at my age, labouring up the hill and into the wind at Checkendon for eight overs should have been grounds for a one off bonus (deduct 25 per cent of runs conceded from my bowling?).

It would not be politic to talk about pensions, as this might embarrass a number of our members who are on the wrong side of the corporate statutory retirement age. At Turville, retirement is only mandatory when you are no longer able to put your pads on unaided. If you think this is overstating my case, it is interesting to look at the Rules designed for the National Village Cricket Knockout Competition which we encountered in Chapter 5. A player who has played more than one First Class game of cricket is ineligible to play in this village competition. Fair enough. Until he reaches 60, when he is effectively 'reborn' as a cricketer, and can take part again. And what a lovely thing that is.

There are other parallels with the business world which might be worth exploring at greater length. Perhaps we could find a former Enron accountant to help us with scoring? I would be surprised if this didn't help us to 'win' more games. Not only is Turville's current scorer, Sara, a lawyer with meticulous attention to detail, but she is married to our Treasurer, 'Colin the Exemplary'. And what about expanding Turville's power base through some aggressive Mergers and Acquisitions? One can only imagine the bloodshed involved in the coming together of the two nearby villages of Nettlebed and Swyncombe. We certainly have enough lawyers and accountants to do the necessary dirty work. Finally, in line with prevailing corporate fashion, we should probably think hard about a 'Vision and Mission Statement'. You may know the type of meaningless and unachievable stuff that gets trotted out -

'Turville is dedicated to raising world cricket standards for the benefit of all stakeholders, while carefully protecting the environment'.

After careful thought, it is more likely that we should run with something like -

'Turville is dedicated to good cricket which finishes by 7.30pm, so we can get to the pub on time'.

But finally, the acid test must always be *results* in the Corporate world. It is therefore only natural to look to the annual batting and bowling awards for recognition of one's contribution to Turville's overall well being. After winning the batting average in my second year with Turville in 2002, I should perhaps have been better prepared for my first innings of Season 2003 at Checkendon. Many of my team mates and batting partners suffered from inexplicable confusion in the judgement of singles, and I found myself on the wrong end of the dreaded 'Yes, No ... Sorry' call. This from Barnaby (the winner of the 2000 batting average, incidentally), who went on to make a very composed 50 not out. Barnaby, I should point out, has a very precise mind. His going away gift from the Singapore Cricket Club was an ancient Club bat, carefully doctored to have a calculator inserted on the reverse side.

We did manage to win our opening game, and 'Turville plc' was set fair to sail on the 2003 Financial Year. But perhaps at last I was beginning to expose the dark and seamy underside of village cricket ...?

·17·

Wormsley - A Class Act
Turville's Annual Intra Club Match,
Players v. Vice-Presidents
Saturday, 30 August, 2003

'My formula for success is rise early, work late,
and strike oil.' **J. Paul Getty**

This quote has nothing to do with the following chapter,
other than the fact that it was uttered by the father of the late
owner of Wormsley Estate, where Turville is privileged to
play its annual intra Club game. I also happen to love the
sentiment. Sometimes I feel like I struck oil when I fell in
with the Turville Park Cricket Club.

Every year, Turville holds what might be termed a
'Players v. Patrons' match at Wormsley Estate. The Turville
'patrons' are largely non-playing supporters of the Club,
also known as 'Vice-Presidents' (a strangely American
'Investment Bank' title for this group of landed gentry). The
Vice-Presidents (or VP's) are the local 'great and good',
and include Sir John Mortimer (Rumpole of the Bailey
fame), Jeremy Paxman (the BBC political presenter - for
Australians, a sort of a Ray Martin with teeth. And intellect.
And gravitas), and Battle of Britain Squadron Leader, and
Chairman Emeritus Air Chief Marshal Sir Christopher

Foxley-Norris. Sir Christopher has been almost single-handedly responsible for assembling such a worthy array of supporters in the VP's group.

Forget everything we've talked about up until now, this is a fixture where it is absolutely crucial to engineer a full day of cricket, in which everyone is able to make a meaningful contribution. Intriguingly, a real result is regarded as important for this intra club match, although not for our 'competitive' games during the season. None of this namby pamby Declaration Cricket stuff and nonsense at Wormsley. And why?....because anything other than a win for one of the teams would simply not be memorable. Here was an illustrious fixture, which demanded a famous result. Like last years tie, on the last ball, in fading light. It was also, of course, a famous social occasion, fully catered for, with specially erected marquees around the ground. More than 100 people turned up to share the silver service lunch.

The cricket pitch at Wormsley Estate was created in 1991 by John Paul Getty II on his estate in Buckinghamshire. Many people will be familiar with the remarkable story of Getty (divided family, kidnapped son, descent into drugs and alcoholism), but it is the influence of cricket on the rehabilitation of this American scion which is especially heartwarming. With the help of friends and cricket buffs like Mick Jagger, Getty fell completely for the game of cricket. So completely, that he became the owner of the games' bible, Wisden, as well as the beautifully imagined and crafted cricket ground at his Wormsley property, said to be modelled on The Oval. It is a very special venue, and is probably as close to a cricket 'time capsule' as you could ever want in order to preserve the great traditions of the game, and hand them down to the next generation. The ground regularly hosts Touring Test teams, and other luminaries, but for one special day each year Turville was lucky enough to enjoy this special facility. Given the sad passing of Mr. Getty, we were not certain if 2003 might be the last time we would be privileged to stage our heroic battle at Wormsley.

Notwithstanding the illustrious Vice-President roll call, the preponderance of public school pedigrees, and the large number of landlords and professionals, I must admit that there has not been even the slightest hint of class warfare at Turville. There are no pretensions, no affectations and little formality. It is a Club which is very much at ease with itself. It was G.M. Trevelyan who suggested (just a little piously) in his 1942 'English Social History' that -

'If the French noblesse had been capable of playing cricket with their peasants their Chateaux would never have been burnt.'

It was perhaps more surprising that there was still some awkwardness about dealing with antipodeans, who are generally stereotyped as aggressive, raw and simple. When we first arrived, it was quite fun to watch these images collapsing within about five seconds of my new team mates meeting Ruth (maybe slightly longer for me, but not much). To be fair, it is hard to blame the English, who (Australia-wise) are fed a diet of arrogant cricketers (who are all assumed to have the etiquette of Shane Warne on the mobile phone), inane suburban 'dramas', and other media driven oddities (of the type - 'Bushtucker Man Eaten By Crocodile in the Bungle Bungles While Searching For German Backpackers').

In fact, the 'cultural' and environmental differences between all three of my 'home' clubs have been remarkably few. There are the obvious ones like afternoon tea, and playing conditions, and weather. And there are those you might expect, like the nature of conversations on the boundary line during a game (at Turville I was regrettably forced to spend more time defending Australia's efforts at Rugby Union, than bagging the English at cricket). Also, at Turville's Trivia Night, I struggled to identify things like a well known mid-60s BBC Sports show tune (Ruth was, however, the only one on our table to know that Lady Jane Grey followed Edward VI to the throne in 1553 - a telling triumph for mid-suburban education in 1970s Australia). But otherwise, my admission into the Turville family had been seamless, and very, very easy. Cricket provided admission to an English community which might otherwise have taken many years to find.

I have become especially fond of the Englishmen I have met and played with at Turville. While they do carry the burden of a long and noble heritage, they invariably manage to do it graciously. And with whimsy - a disarming attribute which the English enjoy and employ like no other country. Self-deprecation is often a key component of this whimsy, but it is neither necessary nor essential. Irony is also of course an important stock-in-trade, but more than anything the English excel at two things - irreverence ('piss-taking' in the vernacular), and sharpness. Their humour (and conversation more generally) is very, very quick witted. While I am leery of pursuing pop psychology too far, I think it is down to the English education system. Children (including my own) are expected from a very early age (through exams in particular, and teacher influence more generally) to become both mature and independent. I happen to think it is a good thing.

The 'burden' of the English which I referred to earlier is best captured in the following passage from Bill Bryson's much loved 'Notes From A Small Island' -

'Here is a country that fought and won a noble war, dismantled a mighty empire in a generally benign and enlightened way, created a far seeing welfare State - in short did nearly everything right - and then spent the rest of the century looking on itself as a chronic failure ... The fact is, this is still the best place in the world for most things - to post a letter, go for a walk, watch TV, buy a book, venture out for a drink, get lost, seek help, or stand on a hillside and take in the view'.

And, Bill might easily have added, if he wasn't an American, 'to play cricket'. (He might also rethink the whole TV thing. It's awful.)

As an Australian, I sometimes feel like the member of a very modern, and very well equipped Southern Hemisphere sports and recreation club, to which I can always return. I count myself extremely lucky that I can safely appreciate and enjoy the best of Englishness, without the complicated baggage of Empire and Europe, which I suspect many English instinctively feel the need to defend or explain (it's worth remembering, for example, that the International Cricket Conference was originally known as the Imperial Cricket Conference).

The combination of English whimsy, the 'burden' of the Englishman's heritage, and their worldly maturity, provides the best explanation I can offer for the hugely depressing fact that Australia has no real equivalent to English village cricket. Even more disheartening, Australia is not likely to generate one (unless perhaps we build an empire of our own? I know there must be many who harbour a secret desire to annexe New Zealand, if for no other reason than to secure access to their Rugby talent pool). And while the Australian 'system' will go on producing hyper-competitive, and no doubt hyper-successful, cricketers, there is a huge generation of cricket lovers over the age of, say, 35, who forsake 20 or more years of playing the game, because there is no vehicle like village cricket in Australia to accommodate them.

At Turville there was the simple shared spirit of fellowship of a unique calling. On this day at Wormsley, there was also the same shared view that surely the captain couldn't be putting the opposition in to bat again after having won the toss. But he did. Our Club Chairman, and VP captain for the day, Andrew Ingram, accepted the invitation with unseemly haste. Of course it didn't really make much difference today at Wormsley, as we were all focussed on getting a full and competitive day's cricket in … and maybe just one more Pimm's before we started.

Batting first, the Vice Presidents XI made a very handsome 219 on a first class pitch from their 45 overs. The innings was anchored by a stylish 95 from Clive Seigal, who knew that the best run scoring opportunities would come directly after our one and a half hour lunch break. Clive dined modestly, and subsequently scored heavily.

In reply, the Players XI cruised to 151-1, with Martin Fennell and Robert Gunn in complete control. At this point, the Players remembered the script, and we contrived to lose our remaining nine wickets for just 53 runs. Fifteen runs short with just three balls remaining in the match. A famous, and fully deserved win for our patrons. The VP's bowling was guided home by a Turville father and son team, Simon and Adam O'Reilly.

I fully expect the VP's 2004 Subscription notices will arrive in the mail this week. Flushed with their success, hopefully they won't notice (or won't care) that we are stinging them for another £50 each next year.

•

John Paul Getty II died in 2003 at age 70, having earned a reputation as a country gentleman, and philanthropist (giving away a reported £100m of his inheritance over his lifetime). His funeral was held at the Stonor Park chapel, where this reclusive man had celebrated Mass on a regular basis. (So that explained Stonor's consistent run of good form.) It is perhaps fitting that his legacy includes not just the magnificent shrine to the game of cricket at Wormsley, but a remarkable capacity to appreciate the grace and charm of this quite foreign (for him) pastime as a means for guiding his personal life, and in particular his generosity of spirit.

I can't think of a more fitting way to end.

ISBN 141202608-3